FULHA
NUMBER
ONES

A CENTURY OF
COTTAGE KEEPERS

Chris Mason

Foreword by Jim Stannard
Illustrations by Bob Armsby

First Published in 1998 by

NORTHDOWN PUBLISHING LIMITED
PO Box 49, Bordon
Hants GU35 0AF

British Library Cataloguing-in-Publication Data
A catalogue for this book is available from the British Library

1 900711 03 6

Designed by Ian Welch
Cover designed by Simon Joslin

PICTURE CREDITS
Photographs in this book have been reproduced courtesy of Ken Coton, Ken Simpson, Yvonne Simpson and Mike Floyd. While every effort has been made to trace the owners of photographs used, this has sometimes proved impossible: such copyright owners are invited to contact the publishers.

Also available from Northdown Publishing:
Rhinos, Winos & Lunatics!
The Legend Of Man
by Deke Leonard
ISBN 1 900711 00 1

Down By The Jetty
The Dr Feelgood Story
by Tony Moon
ISBN 1 900711 01 X

Streets Of London
The Official Ralph McTell Biography
by Chris Hockenhull
ISBN 1 900711 02 8

Pictured right: Hugh Kelly.

CONTENTS

FOREWORD

I was very pleased to be asked to write a few words at the start of this book. Fulham Football Club has always been very special to me, and I remember my years there with great affection.

As many of you will know, I left Fulham twice – in 1985, when I moved to Southend, and again in 1995 when I went to Gillingham – but my heart has always been at Craven Cottage. I had some marvellous times there. The fans were simply terrific and I am only sorry that we did not win anything while I was a Fulham player. At times we had a pretty good side, but the success just would not come.

It's strange, really. I was part of promotion-winning sides at both my other clubs but I never really wanted to go to either of them! I joined Southend because I was 22 and knew that I needed to get regular first-team football. Things went well for me there, but I was more than happy to return home to the Cottage. Things were good at Gillingham too, but promotion at the end of 1995-96 brought with it a certain amount of sadness. We were celebrating at, of all places, Craven Cottage. The Gillingham fans were cheering the team, including me, and I had a lovely reception from the Fulham fans as well. This just made things worse, as I could not help wishing that it was Fulham that was going up – and that I was their keeper.

Whenever the results come through, the first one I look for is Fulham's. I reckon it always will be. I hope you all enjoy reading this book about Fulham goalkeepers. I never realised there had been so many but I can say with all honesty that I am proud to have been one of them.

Jim Stannard

Jim Stannard

INTRODUCTION

This book attempts to tell the stories of goalkeepers who have played for Fulham Football Club since entry into the Second Division of the Southern League was gained in 1898. Not covered – although one or two may receive a passing mention – are goalkeepers who made no first team appearances, or who played for Fulham only in wartime fixtures.

That still leaves a total of 60 brave (and sometimes seemingly insane) custodians who, between them, faced opponents from Maidenhead United on 10 September 1898 to Bristol City on 28 December 1997. In all, they have played in more than four thousand League and Cup matches and conceded more than five and a half thousand goals. Fortunately, they've saved quite a few as well.

Every Fulham supporter knows that Fulham is a great club. It goes without saying, of course. It must however be admitted that the greatness relates more to the ambience of Craven Cottage, plus the fact that, over the years, there have actually been a number of truly great players on Fulham's books, rather than to spectacular achievements by the team as a whole. A glance at some of the contemporary reports on Fulham matches played during the earlier part of this century indeed reveals that goalkeepers were often praised for ensuring that relatively narrow defeats did not become resounding ones. Even so, the club has a long and fascinating history, and it has earned the affection of football fans across the country and beyond.

As everyone with an interest in football is aware, the Fulham story of recent years has been one of turmoil and doubt, with interludes of hope thrown in just to confuse us all. Not long after work started on the compilation of this book came news of the dawning of a new age, with Jimmy Hill relinquishing the chairmanship and Mohamed Al Fayed taking over and promising to restore the fortunes of the club. Hope springs eternal in the Fulham breast, but few could have foreseen the changes that came in such rapid succession thereafter.

Above: Maik Taylor, the man in possession as 1998 started.

The Riverside Stand was suddenly full of seats (thus disproving the rumour that it was Fulham's intention to be the only all-standing club in the League). Micky Adams and Alan Cork, who did so much to lead us out of the depths of Division Three, departed in favour of Kevin Keegan and Ray Wilkins, and newly-signed players began to appear on what seemed an almost daily basis. South African international goalkeeper Andre Arendse was signed during the Adams reign, but the new managerial partnership soon signed Maik Taylor as well, thus ensuring that the side had as much goalkeeping cover as many a Premiership club.

Maik is currently Fulham's first choice, and looks to be on his way to adding another chapter to the long and honourable history of Craven Cottage custodians. And who knows – in the years to come we may yet see an England keeper playing Premiership football down by the Thames.

Chris Mason

ACKNOWLEDGMENTS

The history of Fulham Football Club is already well documented, with Dennis Turner, Alex White, and photographer supreme Ken Coton having previously devoted a great deal of time and energy to what is, quite naturally, a labour of love.

Without the enormous amount of research already undertaken, it would have been impossible to produce this small addition to the Fulham story. The author therefore wishes to thank Dennis, Alex and Ken in particular, and also to acknowledge the help given, and contributions made, by many others.

These include: Alan Barrett, Les Barrett, Ian Black, Peter Carrie, Mike Craig, Tim Craig, Perry Digweed, Dave Gardner, Tony Gale, Olive Haines, Lee Harrison, Brenda Hemmings, Paul Hooper, Bob Howes, Ray Lewington, David Lloyd, John Martin, Dylan Mason, Gillian Mason, Paul McCue, Simon Morgan, Gerry Peyton, John Ryan, Jim Sims, Jim Stannard, Les Strong, Les Strong's Mum, Maik Taylor, Ian Thomas, Martin Townsend, John Vaughan, Arthur Vincent, Mark Walton, Reg Weller and Ray Wilkins.

The statistics provided in this book cover only Southern League (including test matches), Football League (including play-offs), FA Cup and Football League Cup matches. No attempt has been made to include statistics relating to wartime games, strange-sounding competitions which have come and gone, or to games played in the Full Members and Associate Members Cups (under their various commercially sponsored guises). Had the last two been included, it would have caused confusion in the table dealing with consecutive appearances, as reserve keepers have often been used in the early stages of these competitions.

Left: Perry Digweed claims the ball from a watching Terry Mancini.

This contribution to the history of Fulham Football Club is dedicated to the memory of Ted Mason (1906-77), Bob Craig (1922-84), Colin Cunningham (1946-96) and all Fulham supporters who are watching from the great Cottage in the sky.

FULHAM'S FINEST

The eighteen goalkeepers featured in this section all made at least 55 first-team appearances. Some of them, including Arthur Reynolds, Ernie Beecham, Tony Macedo, Peter Mellor, Gerry Peyton and Jim Stannard, gave outstanding service.

All eighteen naturally attracted their share of criticism during their time at Craven Cottage but all of them, including one or two who quite often induced paroxysms of despair among the Fulham faithful, made a valuable contribution to the story of an unique football club.

ERNIE BEECHAM

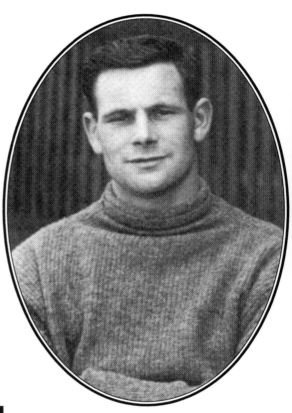

When you ask older Fulham supporters to name a goalkeeper from before the war, they inevitably come up with the name of Ernie Beecham. Some will tell you that he was the greatest of them all, while others will feel a sense of disloyalty to the great Ernie as they reluctantly agree that Tony Macedo also merits consideration for the title. Despite this, no-one has ever been known to seriously question the brilliance and commitment of Ernest Cromwell Beecham.

Ernie Beecham was born in Hertford in July 1906 and made his first-team debut for Fulham in December 1925. He joined his local side, Hertford Town, after the First World War and signed for Fulham in October 1923, turning professional six months later. He was just 19 when he took over from Len Boot and Tom McKenna, neither of whom had proved to be an adequate replacement for Arthur Reynolds between the posts.

MATCH ACTION

**PORT VALE 7 FULHAM 1
(2 APRIL 1927):**
Port Vale gave Fulham a lesson in tactics and adaptability, on a ground which was a sea of mud.

Fulham were inferior in every department save in goal, where Beecham saved his side from worse disaster.

**FULHAM 2 NOTTS COUNTY 1
(10 DECEMBER 1927):**
Beecham has often been acclaimed the hero of the Fulham supporters. He kept goal well in this game too, but marred the exhibition by repeatedly putting goal-kicks among the onlookers.

Ernie's debut came on 5 December 1925, at Blackpool. Fulham lost 2-0, but Ernie was in the side a week later when the Cottagers entertained Port Vale and drew 3-3. Not perhaps the most auspicious start for a former third-choice keeper, but clean sheets in the next two games must have helped to restore any lost confidence.

Ernie was already proving to be a very good goalkeeper but the Fulham side as a whole was struggling in Division Two. Goals at the other end were the main problem, only 53 being scored in the 47 League and Cup games played in 1925-26. The following season was little better (62 in 44 matches) while 1927-28 saw Fulham relegated to the Third Division (South). Remarkably, Ernie did not miss a single game from his debut in 1925 until he

Ernie Beecham was an exceptional goalkeeper. He made some miraculous saves during his career with Fulham, and the supporters loved him. He never appeared upset when fouled and always conducted himself like a gentleman. I was at the game against Exeter in 1928 when he received a severe injury caused by, of all people, a man called Death. Although Ernie continued to play for us after that, I think the injury was a blow to his confidence because he was never quite the same goalkeeper again.

Reg Weller,
Fulham supporter since 1917

A replay at a snow-covered Cottage on a Thursday afternoon was the prize, and Ernie was Fulham's saviour. Henry White scored the only goal of the game, and Ernie 'showed both a coolness and a judgment that many a man of twice his experience might be proud to possess'. Fulham fans carried their hero from the field; a hero who had defied the might of Everton – Dixie Dean and all – and given them an afternoon to remember.

But Ernie had not quite finished with Merseyside. In the Fourth Round, Fulham faced Liverpool at the Cottage, and duly dispatched them 3-1 before travelling to Notts County (another First Division side) where Ernie kept a clean sheet and Bill Prouse scored the winner. Dreams of Wembley glory faded for Ernie Beecham when Manchester United were the Sixth Round visitors and forced two past him, but no-one was left in any doubt about the Fulham goalkeeper's abilities.

Details of the injury which almost ended Beecham's career are a little confused: a broken neck, severe spinal injury, 11 cracked ribs and a punctured lung were all reported,

suffered a serious injury in November 1928, and one wonders just how much worse Fulham's record would have been during those sad seasons had he not been their formidable custodian.

As it was, the side achieved some very unusual results during Ernie's 130 consecutive appearances. A 6-2 victory over Port Vale in November 1926 was followed by a 6-1 defeat at Middlesbrough within seven days, while later that season Ernie conceded five goals in three consecutive matches (against Barnsley, Manchester City and Darlington). Later still, Port Vale put seven past him, as did Nottingham Forest in the second game of the 1927-28 campaign. In January 1928, Fulham went down 8-4 at Barnsley, but a few days later walloped Wolves 7-0.

Ernie Beecham was an heroic goalkeeper – he needed to be, given the League performances of some of his team-mates in the mid to late 1920s – but his finest hour probably came during Fulham's FA Cup run of 1926, not long after his League debut. It sometimes happens that a team which struggles in the League will experience a run of success in the Cup, and so it was with Fulham during 1925-26.

The Cottagers were struggling (unsuccessfully) to reach a mid-table position in Division Two when they were drawn to play Everton in the Third Round. As ever, they were given little chance but managed to surprise the Alan Hansens of the day by drawing 1-1 in front of 46,000 Merseysiders.

He's 50 years of age now, and physically nothing like the man for whom thousands of our supporters had a warm place in their hearts, but Ernie Beecham's name is still a household word in many Fulham homes. He is remembered not only as a very fine goalkeeper, but also as a keeper who might well have achieved great heights but for the serious injuries he suffered. People still talk of the tremendous length he could kick a ball.

Extract from a Fulham
programme 40 years ago

**PORTSMOUTH 0 FULHAM 0
(2 APRIL 1926):**
Portsmouth had one splendid chance in the first half, when Mackie, with only the goalkeeper to beat, failed with a pass from Martin.

In the second half, when the Portsmouth forwards warmed to their work, Beecham proved the saviour of the side, and at the conclusion was carried off shoulder-high by a band of visiting supporters. There was no doubt that his display warranted such an honour.

and it is certainly true that the result of his death-defying dive in a game against Exeter City in November 1928 was a matter of great concern for everyone connected with Fulham FC. Ernie was a brave man, however, and he was back on duty at the start of the following season, keeping a clean sheet against Norwich City.

He made 40 first-team appearances during that 1929-30 season, helping Fulham to seventh place in the Third Division (South) table. His appearances were limited after that, and his last game for Fulham was at Reading on 3 October 1931, a month after he had let in two at Torquay – while his team-mates were scoring ten at the other end. Ironically, Fulham were to finish top of the table in May 1932. Ernie would have loved to have been a part of that.

FULHAM RECORD	
Seasons Played:	1925-32
Total Appearances:	185
Goals Conceded:	357
Average Per Match:	1.929
Clean Sheets:	41 (22%)
One Goal Conceded:	40 (22%)
Two or More Conceded:	104 (56%)
Most Conceded:	8 v Barnsley, 28 Jan 1928, Div 2

Ernie Beecham moved to Queens Park Rangers in the month that Fulham became Champions, before breaking his arm and deciding to retire. He came out of retirement to join Brighton, transfered to Swindon, and then finally did retire in March 1936. He suffered as a result of his injuries for the rest of his life, but lived until 1985.

Top: Ernie Beecham and his wife Florence pictured in 1984, at home in Hertford.

IAN BLACK

'**E**xcellent anticipation and a safe pair of hands are two of his many fine attributes.' That was how *Soccer Star* described Ian Black in August 1953.

By the time he was featured in that article, Ian was well established as Fulham's principal goalkeeper, having taken over from Doug Flack at the commencement of the 1950-51 season. Born in Aberdeen in March 1924, Ian began his professional career with his home city club but, as the war was still in progress, he was able to make guest appearances with both Chelsea (where he won a League South Cup winner's medal) and Southampton.

After the hostilities, Ian returned to Aberdeen but, when he later lost his place in the first team, he was signed by Southampton. This was in 1947 and it was while he was at the Dell that he earned his one and only cap, keeping a clean sheet in a Scottish 2-0 victory over England at Hampden Park. In the summer of 1950 Fulham manager Bill Dodgin, who had previously been in charge of affairs at Southampton, signed him in a player-exchange deal involving Hugh Kelly. Ian went straight into Fulham's Division One side and was ever-present in his first season.

Tall and stylish, but with just a hint of vulnerability on crosses, Black had joined a side struggling to retain First Division status. He did well in that first season although, at a time when relatively few people travelled to away games, some Fulham supporters were probably less than impressed with his performances. Away from

FULHAM RECORD	
Seasons Played:	1950-58
Total Appearances:	277
Goals Conceded:	471
Average Per Match:	1.700
Clean Sheets:	48 (17%)
One Goal Conceded:	97 (35%)
Two or More Conceded:	132 (48%)
Most Conceded:	6 v Leeds United, 2 Apr 1956, Div 2 6 v Blackpool, 26 Jan 1957, FAC

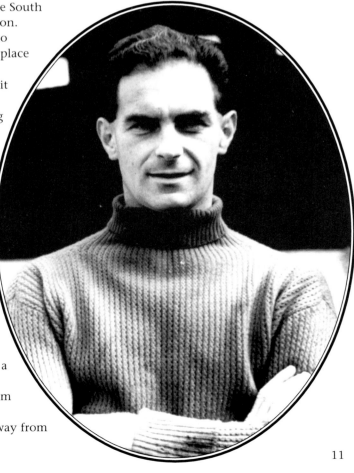

home the Fulham defence conceded only 31 League goals, while at the Cottage the ball passed Ian by on 37 occasions. He kept only two clean sheets at home, recording five on away territory.

With full-backs Harry Freeman and Joe Bacuzzi approaching the end of their careers, Fulham finished the 1950-51 season in 18th place. They did, however, reach the Sixth Round of the FA Cup, conceding only one goal in four games on their way to a 1-0 defeat at Blackpool. A 3-0 home win in the Fifth Round replay over Chelsea – where Ian was mainly occupied in retrieving the ball after Chelsea had missed the target – was followed by the game at Bloomfield Road in which he had a lot more to do. As journalist Tom Markland reported at the time:

'Black's anticipation saved the Fulham goal time and time again in the second half, but how some chances-on-a-plate openings created by a

FIRST PERSON

Another player's impatience started me on the road to big football. This is how it happened...

In my schooldays, at Aberdeen, I used to play for a very scratch Boys' Brigade team. Our matches were easy going affairs and if we couldn't muster a team, we turned out with as many as we had! I was younger than the other boys but was willing to play anywhere in the team for a game.

Our performances were no more successful than our organisation. We usually retired beaten by ten or 11 goals and one day, in a fit of pique, our goalkeeper decided he had had enough. As I was jack-of-all-positions, the goalie's jersey was flung at me, and from that moment I've stayed between the posts.

It was a good job I linked up with the Boys' Brigade team. When they turned me into a goalkeeper I was given all the work an aspiring young player could expect!

Ian Black writing in
Football Monthly, April 1952

Matthews at his best were missed passeth all understanding.'

Ian was, however, beaten by a penalty, and the run was at an end.

The 1951-52 League campaign saw Ian miss just three games through injury as Fulham finished bottom of the table. It was a sad but inevitable season in which a run of 11 games without a win between 9 February and 19 April sealed the side's fate. Home wins over Huddersfield and Derby County at the campaign's end, in which Ian kept his goal intact, were to prove of little consequence as Fulham returned to Division Two.

The Cottagers made a bright start to 1952-53 by beating Bury 2-0, but then travelled to Leicester City where Black became the first Fulham goalkeeper to score a goal. His side lost 6-1, due to the fact that Ian was injured and was forced to quit the goalmouth in favour of the role of centre-forward. Following this injury he missed two games, and then returned for the majority of a season which saw Fulham finish in eighth place.

Over the next four campaigns, Ian suffered a number of injuries – including a broken arm – which restricted his appearances. Even so, he featured in 130 Division Two games between

1953-54 and 1956-57. Fulham mostly finished in mid-table positions during this time, thanks mainly to great feats of goalscoring by Beddy Jezzard and, later, Roy Dwight, but the defence was not always at its best.

A highlight for Ian came at the end of the period when he kept four clean sheets in a row, but there were one or two disasters along the way. Perhaps the 5-4 beating by Newcastle in a Fourth Round FA Cup match in January 1956 hardly rates as a disaster, as this is widely recognised as one of the finest games ever witnessed at the Cottage, but a 6-1 defeat at Elland Road in April of that year may still give Ian the occasional nightmare.

The 1957-58 season saw the emergence of Tony Macedo. A 2-1 victory over Huddersfield in November 1957 was to be Ian's last game at Craven Cottage and in August 1959 he moved to Southern League Bath City. He later coached Brentford's juniors, and then abandoned football to manage an indoor bowls club.

When he left the Cottage, there was a certain amount of acrimony between Ian Black and Fulham Football Club. Ian is alive and well and living in Tolworth, but has never returned to the club at which he made his name.

DOUG FLACK

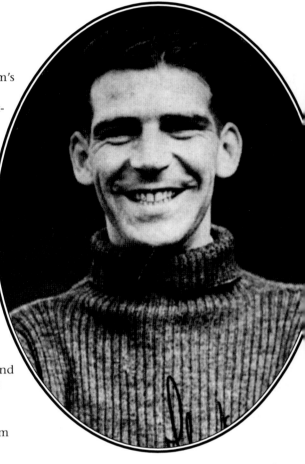

Doug Flack was one of Fulham's unluckier goalkeepers in terms of the number of first-team appearances he was able to make. Born in Staines in October 1920, he later won a scholarship to Spring Grove Grammar School where he came under the influence of the great Bernard Joy, who was a teacher at the school.

Bernard was a former amateur international and Arsenal centre-half who also played one League game for Fulham in 1934, and when he went to Craven Cottage to train for the 1936 Olympic Games he took the youngster along with him. Doug was already building a reputation as a school goalkeeper and he stayed on at Fulham – as an office boy!

He soon got a chance to play, however, and when he kept goal for the first team against Cambridge University and Corinthians in friendly matches he was believed to be the youngest player ever to appear in the Fulham senior side. By 1939 he was ready for his

FAN'S EYE VIEW

Whoever said 'To get promotion from the lower leagues you need a fearless goalie, a granite centre-half and a greedy centre-forward – plus eight others who will die for their manager' must have got it right as far as Fulham in 1948-49 was concerned.

Duggie Flack, Jim Taylor and Arthur Rowley were the three in question. Comparisons are odious, but I like to think that at times during 1996-97 we had Tony Lange, Simon Morgan and Mick Conroy as their modern counterparts, with eight Darren Freemans making up the team.

We hammered QPR 5-0 on Doug's debut on 2 October 1948 and he helped to keep us in the top four all the way through to Easter Monday at Luton, where we completed a wonderful treble in four days, setting ourselves up to become eventual Champions.

Doug Flack suffered a very bad injury in the second Luton game and arguably was never quite the same. But he was the goalkeeper who took us up to the First Division for the first time.

Jim Sims (aka Lilliewhite), a Fulham fan
since the war years

League debut, but war clouds had gathered and major footballing ambitions had to be put on hold. Doug played as a guest keeper for a number of London sides between 1939 and 1942, and also played for the Football Association three times.

In 1942, Doug joined the RAF and spent three years in the Far East, during which time he toured India, Burma, Malaya and Singapore with a team formed in Delhi from professional players in the Services.

When he was demobbed in 1946 he returned to the Cottage to find that Fulham already had four goalkeepers on their books. Even though one of these was the massive Ossie Evans, it soon became clear to Doug that first-team opportunities would be at a premium.

He persevered, though, and his debut finally came in October 1948. Fulham had won only three of their first ten games at the start of that campaign, and were languishing near the foot of the Second Division table. Doug was brought in to replace Ted Hinton who, although he probably didn't know it at the time, had played his last game for the Cottagers.

Below: Doug Flack pictured in training with the Putney End behind him.

COTTAGE COMMENT

Douglas Flack has every right to be called one of Fulham's old faithfuls. He has been with the club ever since he left school. He worked in the club's office before he was 16 years old, after he had given great promise in his schoolboy days of being a fine goalkeeper.

Extract from the programme for the game against Huddersfield on 26 April 1952

Fulham's former office boy kept a clean sheet in that first match, a much appreciated 5-0 victory over Queens Park Rangers, and went on to give some spectacular performances between the posts, although a great deal of credit for defending must also be given to Harry Freeman and Joe Bacuzzi.

Fulham were to finish the season as Second Division Champions, Bob Thomas, Arthur Rowley and Arthur Stevens the marksmen with 54 goals between them, and Doug Flack conceding just 21 times in 30 League and Cup appearances. He even helped Fulham gain revenge over Bury, by letting in two while Rowley (4), Thomas (2) and Jack McDonald helped themselves to seven, to produce a mirror image of the scoreline at Gigg Lane on the first day of the first postwar season.

Doug missed the last three games of the 1948-49 campaign after breaking his jaw in a 3-1 victory at Luton. In 1984 he recalled the incident, when he made the mistake of answering the door to the intrepid Lilliewhite:

'That was my Waterloo, the return game at Luton. Five minutes to go, we're holding on to our narrow lead and Bircumshaw gets clean through.

'Out I come for what I think is a fifty-fifty ball and bang, a broken jaw. I was wired up for two and a half months and had operations involving dental and orthopaedic surgery – the lot.'

During that interview, Doug also recalled a couple of penalty saves that he made during the glorious campaign:

'The first was against Lincoln at the Cottage, and it was Jock Dodds. He hammered it to my left but I just got it round the post for a corner. The second was at Hillsborough and Whitcomb slammed the ball in the corner past me, with no problem at all. It would have been a last-second equaliser and cost us a vital point.

'Luckily Harry Freeman, who had conceded it, was still swearing and cursing to himself just inside the area. The ref spotted that and for some reason, known only to himself, ordered a retake. I kept my eyes on Whitcomb in the mayhem and the Wednesday skipper came right up to him and breathed "Put it in the same place." Luckily he did, and I was there. Tommy Trinder came rushing on the pitch and slung his arms around me, and shortly afterwards I received a silver cigarette box from him, with the words "With admiration Doug – Tommy Trinder" inscribed on it.'

Jock Dodds later described the first of those two saves as the finest he had ever seen, and no doubt Harry Freeman felt the same about the second.

Doug had, more or less, recovered from his broken jaw by the start of the following season, but from then on his first-team appearances were to be restricted. Ian Black was eventually to take over his duties and Doug played his last League game for Fulham in January 1953 (a 0-0 draw at Doncaster). He moved to Walsall and ceased playing League football at the age of 34.

He took up coaching and led Corinthian Casuals to an FA Amateur Cup Final before moving to Tooting and Mitcham as manager in 1964. Doug Flack finally retired from football in 1970.

FULHAM RECORD	
Seasons Played:	1948-50, 1951-53
Total Appearances:	55
Goals Conceded:	67
Average Per Match:	1.218
Clean Sheets:	15 (27%)
One Goal Conceded:	24 (44%)
Two or More Conceded:	16 (29%)
Most Conceded:	6 v Leicester City, 3 Sep 1952, Div 2

JACK FRYER

'Jack Fryer beams like a sun, though he is only a star' wrote a contributor to an early Fulham programme – which, in those days, was known as the *Cottagers' Journal*.

The writer presumably knew rather more about football than he knew about astronomy, but there is no doubt that Jack Fryer dominated the penalty area during the four seasons Fulham spent in the First Division of the Southern League, and is easily the best-known of the goalkeepers from the early days of the club.

A genial character, he was appointed club captain and only a serious injury prevented him from becoming Fulham's first goalkeeper in the Football League when, in 1907, the Cottagers finally attained that status along with Oldham.

It seems likely that Jack found domination of his area fairly easy, as he was a keeper who loomed very large indeed. He was well over six feet tall and weighed in at more than thirteen and a half stone. This, combined with remarkable agility for one so large and an apparently total disregard for his own safety, helped prevent the opposition from scoring in almost half the games in which he stood between the posts.

It also led him to achieve a remarkable rate of 0.835 goals conceded per game – an average which would have been even lower had he not returned from injury after an absence of 20 months to take over, for a while at least, from Leslie Skene.

Jack Fryer was born in Cromford sometime in 1877, and was 26 years old when he joined Fulham. He had played minor league football until signed by Derby County in 1897, where he took part in three FA Cup Finals. The Rams lost all three and Jack, somewhat surprisingly,

conceded 13 goals in the three matches – including six in the 1903 Final against Bury. Derby decided to dispense with his services following the Bury game, and Jack moved south to the club he came to love.

He joined a brand-new Fulham team. Having been admitted to the Southern League's First Division at the start of the 1903-04 season, the club was re-formed as a limited liability company and proceeded to sign several new players.

Clean sheets in his first two games – a draw at home to Tottenham Hotspur and another at Luton, where the Cottagers' new custodian was reported to have made more than 20 saves in the second half – signalled a promising start for Big Jack, and he went on to concede just 32 goals in 28 League appearances.

He was helped by the fact that, in those days, goalkeepers were given much more freedom of movement when a penalty was being taken and Jack's agility, combined with his dimensions, meant that he saved more spot-kicks than most.

The 1903-04 season also saw Fulham enjoy a significant run in the FA Cup, where they reached the First Round proper, having played

nine Qualifying Round matches. Jack was between the posts in seven of these games, and conceded just four goals – the last being the only goal in the First Round game away to Woolwich Arsenal.

The 1904-05 campaign saw Fryer miss just three games (one a 3-0 home defeat by West Ham in which the marvellously named Henry James Clutterbuck deputised) and saw him take part in a record-breaking 12-0 win over Wellingborough. Another run in the FA Cup meant more opportunities for clean sheets, and during the season Jack prevented the opposition from scoring on 23 occasions. He did, however, concede six at Luton and five in the Third Round of the FA Cup at Aston Villa.

The next two seasons saw Jack Fryer miss only six League games, and he continued to frustrate opposing forwards. He was, of course, fortunate that Fulham had a good side during these years, one which won the Southern League Division One title in 1905-06 and 1906-07. Goals were often quite hard to come by, and few games saw the ball enter the net more than three times (it seems nobody told Wellingborough).

Fulham's defence was particularly strong, with Scottish half-backs Billy Goldie and Billy Morrison being virtually ever-present during those two Championship-winning seasons. Formidable contributions also came from half-back Pat Collins and, especially, from full-backs Harry Ross and Harry Thorpe.

Nonetheless, Jack was obviously an excellent goalkeeper. When he returned to the

MATCH ACTION

Jack Fryer's last season saw this newspaper report on a goalless draw at Chesterfield in the First Round of the FA Cup, played on 15 January 1910:

At Chesterfield on Saturday the home team turned out as expected, while the visitors had two changes, Fryer taking the place of RP O'Donnell and Mouncher replacing Lipsham. Fully 9,000 spectators witnessed the game, although rain was falling heavily when play started.

Chesterfield won the toss and Harrison started the ball in motion but was soon driven back by Denby. Immediately after this, Chesterfield made a raid and Stevens when in a good position was pulled up for offside. Shortly afterwards Thacker fouled Brown and the visitors then got going and became dangerous.

A foul was next given against Chesterfield for handling, and Charlton placed the ball in the home goalmouth, causing Martin to concede a corner. This was got away and Denby tested Fryer, the latter saving in brilliant fashion by dropping at full length. Up to half-time the game was very much in favour of Chesterfield but they could not score.

On returning Munday made a fine pass to Owers, who in turn crossed over to Dickie. The last named tried for all he was worth, but failed to get the ball, thus giving a goal-kick.

Fryer was frequently called upon in the closing stages but he stopped all straight shots and the result was a goalless draw.

(Fulham won the replay 2-1.)

team during the 1908-09 season, Fulham were established (not for the last time) as a mid-table Football League Second Division side, and had a rather more leaky defence.

Left: Surveying the action at Elm Park in the First Round of the 1904-05 FA Cup. The season saw Fulham finish sixth in the Southern League and reach the Third Round of the Cup.

Jack Fryer, however, continued to give good service until he retired in 1910 to run a pub near, of all places, Stamford Bridge. He died in 1933.

FULHAM RECORD

Seasons Played:	1903-07, 1908-10
Total Appearances:	170
Goals Conceded:	142
Average Per Match:	0.835
Clean Sheets:	82 (48%)
One Goal Conceded:	54 (32%)
Two or More Conceded:	34 (20%)
Most Conceded:	6 v Luton Town, 7 Jan 1905, SL Div 1

TED HINTON

Ted Hinton joined Fulham in August 1946 and departed for Millwall a little under three years later. He was an accomplished goalkeeper and would in all probability have remained at Craven Cottage for far longer had it not been for the emergence of Doug Flack.

Ted was born in Belfast in May 1922. He began his career with Glentoran, turning professional at the age of 19, and playing for his club in the 1942 Irish Cup Final. He transferred to Distillery a year later and, when they apparently forgot to re-sign him in 1946, was snapped up by Fulham manager Jack Peart.

After Ossie Evans had let in a substantial number of goals in the Cottagers' opening postwar defeat at Bury, Ted entered the fray. Three passed him on his debut at West Ham, but things improved after that and he was in goal for much of the remainder of the season. Fulham were enjoying a somewhat shaky start to football's new age and were to finish in 15th place in the Second Division, but Ted's domination of the penalty area ensured that matters were not far worse.

FIRST PERSON

Jim Sims used to keep a book of Fulham press cuttings and photographs, in which he also made notes. Here is what he wrote about Ted Hinton:
This brilliant goalie really came into prominence last season (1946-47) when, besides playing in over 30 League games for Fulham, he was capped twice for Ireland. Catches the ball and dives extremely well and is not afraid to advance outside the penalty area to stop an onrushing forward.

It was during the early part of the 1946-47 season that Ted won the first of his international caps, keeping a clean sheet in a goalless draw against Scotland played in Glasgow during November. He was to win seven caps in all, five while he was at the Cottage (all Home Internationals) with his only other clean sheet coming once more against Scotland in a 2-0 win in Belfast in October 1947.

Below: Hinton fists away from Everton forward Harry Catterick in this February 1948 FA Cup tie. Fulham progressed to the Sixth Round after a replay.

Jim's scrapbook also contains the following, probably from the *Sunday Express*, part of a report on a goalless draw at Ninian Park in March 1948:

Hinton, the star of the game, has seldom had so many pointblank shots sent straight at him. In one ten-minute spell he saved amazingly from all five Cardiff forwards.

FULHAM RECORD

Seasons Played:	1946-49
Total Appearances:	86
Goals Conceded:	110
Average Per Match:	1.279
Clean Sheets:	24 (28%)
One Goal Conceded:	31 (36%)
Two or More Conceded:	31 (36%)
Most Conceded:	6 v West Brom, 23 Nov 1946, Div 2

Ted was not to remain in the first team long enough to share in Second Division success, but he missed only one League game in the 1947-48 season – a campaign which started brightly with a 5-0 victory over Brentford. The Bees were not buzzing a great deal that season (although in the end they finished on 40 points – the same number as Fulham) and Ted completed his own double over them when the return fixture resulted in a 2-0 win.

Ted Hinton was ably assisted during 1947-48 by the full-back pairing of Harry Freeman and Joe Bacuzzi, and only 46 goals were conceded in 42 League games – a very low number when one considers that the side finished a modest 11th in the table. Ted had a run of five clean sheets in March 1948, somewhat surprisingly while Harry Freeman was out of the side – although Joe was doing his usual sterling stuff at left-back.

These were the good times for Ted. A few weeks earlier he had played a vital part in his side's FA Cup Fifth Round replay at Goodison Park. Having drawn the first encounter 1-1 before a crowd of 37,500, Fulham won 1-0 before a Merseyside audience numbering an incredible 71,587.

Ted was widely praised for turning one particular shot over the bar during a brave performance by the Cottagers – but unfortunately he was missing from the line-up when Fulham entertained Blackpool in the Sixth Round, and lost 2-0.

Ted's last game proved to be a 2-1 home defeat by Cardiff in September 1948. Doug Flack was at last getting his chance, and from then on it was reserve-team football for Ted. He moved to Millwall for a modest fee and went on to make 91 Third Division (South) appearances for the Lions, while his first English side went on to greater glory in Division One.

JAKE ICETON

Jake Iceton was born in West Auckland in October 1903 and, like many of his contemporaries in that part of the world, became a coal miner on leaving school. Like a lot of others, however, he saw professional football as a way of escaping from the drudgery and dangers of mining, so this 'big fellow, who could take the knocks', as he was once described, attempted to hone his goalkeeping skills to perfection and, in 1928, applied to join Hull City.

Hull took him on but, sadly for Jake, they let him go again and he joined Shildon FC. His luck was to change, however, when fellow north-easterner and Fulham manager Ned Liddell decided he would be a likely replacement for the ageing Ernie Beecham. Jake moved to the soft south and signed for the Cottagers in the summer of 1930.

Fulham were beginning another season in the Third Division (South) and everyone was hoping that 1930-31 would prove third time lucky as far as promotion back to the Second was concerned. It was not to be, as the Cottagers finished ninth – their lowest League

FULHAM RECORD	
Seasons Played:	1930-34
Total Appearances:	99
Goals Conceded:	151
Average Per Match:	1.525
Clean Sheets:	25 (25%)
One Goal Conceded:	25 (25%)
Two or More Conceded:	49 (50%)
Most Conceded:	5 v Crystal Palace, 18 Oct 1930, Div 3 S 5 v Luton Town, 1 Nov 1930, Div 3 S 5 v Coventry City, 2 Jan 1932, Div 3 S

Older Fulham supporters tend to glaze over when asked about Jake Iceton. They sort of recall him, but cannot actually remember much about him.

His performances are also less well documented than those of most other Fulham goalkeepers, but here are a few snippets from newspaper reports:

FULHAM 3 WATFORD 2
(30 AUGUST 1930):
Iceton, the new Fulham keeper, was perhaps the weakest spot in the home defence.

FULHAM 2 BRENTFORD 1
(26 DECEMBER 1931):
Ten minutes before the interval Richards got Fulham's first goal with a simple shot, which Smith should have saved. Smith, throughout the match, seemed nervous and he repeatedly rushed out of goal when his backs were well placed for dealing with the Fulham attacks. More impressive was the display of Iceton in the Fulham goal – particularly in the second half, when Brentford had some spells of storming pressure.

FULHAM 3 BRIGHTON 0
(19 MARCH 1932):
This match at Craven Cottage was productive of much fine football, equally good to anything I have seen this season. Fulham, strengthened by Wrightson at inside-right, and Newton in the centre, gave a fast and clever display. Both Iceton and Webb did well, but the back play of either side was not impressive.

position up until that time – but Jake went straight into the side and did well enough.

His first game was a 3-2 home win over Watford and his second a goalless draw at home to Coventry City. Beecham came back for the next fixture, which resulted in a 6-1 hammering at Notts County, so Iceton returned immediately to the fray.

Jake was first-choice keeper for most of the remainder of the season, with Beecham appearing on just five more occasions. He conceded five goals at Crystal Palace in October, and another five at Luton in November, but his season saw a total of ten clean sheets in 40 games, including two in the FA Cup – a 6-0 win in a First Round replay at Wimbledon, and a 4-0 home victory over Halifax in Round Two.

The 1931-32 season saw Beecham play in the first nine games but Jake was ever-present after that in what proved to be the Cottagers' Championship season. It was, naturally enough, a good campaign for Jake Iceton as well. True, he featured in a remarkable 5-5 draw at Coventry played in a sea of mud but, due to the ball getting stuck, he saved a last-minute penalty in that game.

He was also between the posts when Fulham beat Thames 8-0 at the Cottage in March – and followed up this trouncing a few days later with a 5-0 victory over Watford. Fulham were going up, and Jake was going with them.

The following campaign was almost as good for the Cottagers as 1931-32 had been. Jim Hammond and, in particular, Bonzo Newton were scoring freely at the other end and, with Joe Birch at right-back and a half-back line of Len Oliver, Syd Gibbons and Albert Barrett, Fulham were to finish third behind Stoke and Tottenham – only narrowly missing out on further promotion.

The season was not, however, an especially happy one for Jake. He was contented enough for the first 15 games, but then along came Alf Tootill to replace him, and Jake made only four more first-team appearances during that campaign.

Jake Iceton's last League game for Fulham came in April 1934. He had made only one previous appearance during the 1933-34 campaign and bowed out in a 1-0 defeat at Bradford City. He stayed at the Cottage for another year before moving to Aldershot on a free transfer.

He later signed for Clapton Orient, where he played 40 first-team games before retiring due to war. Jake died in 1981.

TONY LANGE

Tony Lange had a long and varied career before he joined Fulham in the summer of 1995. Born in West Ham in December 1964, he supported the Hammers as a boy but his family moved to Orpington and he signed for Charlton Athletic as an apprentice. His first League appearance was on his 19th birthday, when he featured in a 1-0 victory over Fulham at the Cottage.

Tony played only a dozen League games for Charlton before being loaned, and later transferred, to Aldershot, where he made a total of 125 Fourth and Third Division appearances. While at the Recreation Ground he suffered the indignity of seeing Fulham put ten past him in a Freight Rover Trophy match – an indignity matched only by what happened to Johnny Vaughan at the other end, who let in 11. This was of course a penalty-kick decider, and no-one was particularly bothered.

In December 1995 Fulham were perilously near the foot of Division Three. This is what Tony had to say when interviewed by Jonathan Sim for the programme:
We're not in a good position at the moment. But if we win a couple of games we can almost be in a play-off position. The pattern of the season has changed because we were scoring and conceding goals but still winning games. Now we are not conceding many, but not winning.

Having made his mark at Aldershot, Tony Lange moved to Wolverhampton Wanderers for a £150,000 fee in 1989. Sadly, he was unable to make a similar impression at Molineux and in 1992, after a handful of first-team games, he joined Black Country rivals West Bromwich Albion. Fulham secured his services in time for the start of the 1995-96 campaign.

This was a season which saw Fulham reach the nadir of its existence and, as seasons go, it does not bear too much writing about. It actually started very well, but then it became mediocre, and then very bad indeed, before it was finally rescued by the appointment of Micky Adams as team manager. Fulham's, and Tony Lange's, first game of the campaign was a 4-2 home win over Mansfield Town, and Tony followed this up with a clean sheet at the Goldstone Ground, as Fulham beat Brighton 3-0 in the First Round of the Coca-Cola Cup. A 2-2 draw at Scarborough was followed by another clean sheet against Brighton (in the second leg of the 'fizzy drink' competition) and a 4-0 victory over Torquay. Fulham were second in Division Three, and all was right with the world.

The Cottagers then slid rapidly down the table, and very nearly crashed through the floor. Even so, they did not generally concede a large number of goals. It is true that Wolves put five past Tony in the second leg of the next round of the Coca-Cola Cup, and that Lincoln City scored four at Sincil Bank in the League, but in-between times there was an extraordinary clean sheet for Tony as Fulham walloped Swansea 7-0 in the First Round of the FA Cup.

Opposite bottom: In action against Carlisle.

Above: Scoring against Brighton.

FULHAM RECORD	
Seasons Played:	1995-97
Total Appearances:	70
Goals Conceded:	94
Average Per Match:	1.342
Clean Sheets:	18 (26%)
One Goal Conceded:	26 (37%)
Two or More Conceded:	26 (37%)
Most Conceded:	5 v Wolves, 3 Oct 1995, CCC 5 v Plymouth Argyle, 16 Nov 1996, FAC

Shortly after the Swansea triumph, Fulham went to Gillingham and most of the team became involved in a punch-up with the home side. Happily, Lange was not involved. He was, however, very much involved when Fulham again met Brighton, this time in the Second Round of the FA Cup. Having kept a clean sheet in a draw at the Cottage, Tony distinguished himself at the Goldstone Ground and was largely responsible for his team's progression to Round Three, where Fulham went down 2-1 to Shrewsbury after drawing 1-1 at the Cottage.

Many Fulham fans were still pining for Jim Stannard, but there was a feeling of optimism – for once justified – as the 1996-97 season began. Fulham were not, after all, starting it in

the Vauxhall Conference – and, with Micky beginning his first full season as King of the Cottage, everyone hoped and prayed for much better things.

New signing Mark Walton played in the first three games, then Tony had a run of five appearances as Fulham leapt to the top of the table. Mark returned, but when Tony took over again in November the Cottagers were still proudly looking down on everyone else.

They in fact remained on top for the rest of Tony Lange's Fulham career. Between the 2-1 victory at Cardiff on 9 November and the 4-1 defeat at home to the very same side on 31 January, Tony kept four clean sheets – and helped to ensure that promotion was eventually gained. In the circumstances, then, his record is a very good one.

Tony Lange was offered a free transfer at the end of the 1996-97 season and has apparently since worked as a landscape gardener and as a postman in Bognor.

TONY MACEDO

Ask any football supporter to think of a famous Fulham player from times past and, having first come up with the name of Johnny Haynes, he or she may then nominate Tony Macedo. Given that the latter was hailed as one of the finest goalkeeping prospects to emerge during the 1950s, it is perhaps quite surprising that, although he made ten England Under-23 appearances, Tony Macedo never actually won full international honours.

This may in part have been due to what we would today call racism – that very English assumption that all foreigners (even if, like Tony Macedo, they had lived in this country for almost all their lives) were a little odd, or at least rather funny. However, Tony's cause was not helped by the fact that his bravery between the posts led to a number of injuries at crucial times in his goalkeeping life – nor by the fact that he played for a team which, for much of his career, was struggling to maintain First Division status.

Elio Macedo was born in Gibraltar in February 1938, his family moving to north London not long afterwards. Elio had trials for the England Youth side and also represented Middlesex. In 1954 he became an apprentice cabinet-maker, and simultaneously joined the groundstaff at Craven Cottage, where his acrobatic skills made an immediate impression.

He played for the juniors and for the reserve team and signed professional forms in 1956. Cabinet-making was forgotten, but National Service loomed and young Elio joined the RAF. All was well at the Cottage as Ian Black was giving sterling service, but in November 1957 Black was injured and Fulham faced a goalkeeping

Left: Macedo defies League Champions Ipswich in October 1962. The match resulted in a 1--1 draw.

I was a young fan of 13 when I witnessed one of Tony Macedo's brilliant performances. It was on 22 March 1958 in the Semi-Final of the FA Cup against Manchester United. It was only his 20th first-team appearance and he had already established himself as one of the stars of a great Fulham team. His agility, anticipation and courage had helped the team to the Semi-Final, and also to being candidates for promotion to the top division.

In the first half Fulham were 2-1 in the lead and well in control. Then Jim Langley was stretchered off leaving Fulham with ten men, and United drew level. Although Jim came back and played gallantly, Fulham were severely disadvantaged. From my young viewpoint, Manchester United seemed to dominate the whole of a very long second half.

Waves of red shirts descended on the Fulham goal, but each time Tony came away with the ball having made a spectacular save. He saved everything, including two thunderbolts from a young Bobby Charlton, who was made man of the match by the Press. My man of the match, however, was Tony Macedo. He displayed all the qualities of a truly great keeper and took Fulham to a replay at Highbury. But that, of course, is another story.

Fulham fan Mike Craig remembers the first FA Cup game against Manchester United:

crisis. Strings were pulled and the club paid for their young keeper to fly home from his RAF station in Germany to make his debut in a Second Division match at Bristol City on 7 December. Fulham won 5-0 and, presumably after the pulling of a lot more strings, Elio remained in the side for the rest of the season. The Macedo era had begun.

Elio soon became Tony, and established himself as first-choice keeper. He played in 23 League games during that 1957-58 season, and Fulham finished in fifth place. They would probably have done better had it not been for the fixture congestion caused by an extended run in the FA Cup, and it was in the Cup that the real action occurred.

Tony played in all five games leading to the Semi-Final, and conceded just four goals. The Cottagers then faced Manchester United in the wake of the Munich disaster, and Tony acquitted himself brilliantly. Without him, the goals scored by Arthur Stevens and Jimmy Hill would not have been sufficient to secure a replay.

Tony began the replay in fine form too, making three flying saves in the first ten minutes – but then he twice threw the ball out to the feet of United players and these errors, in the end, cost Fulham the tie. The Cottagers lost 5-3, and there was to be no Wembley appearance for Tony Macedo.

Undaunted (and still only 20 years old), Tony helped his team to win nine of the first ten games when the 1958-59 season

26 DECEMBER 1957:

Still, we won – that was the important thing. Also important was the fact that while we were scoring seven goals (five at Bristol City and two at home to Cardiff) Elio Macedo hadn't let one into our net.

He made his League debut at Bristol but was now appearing at the Cottage for the first time. And we reckon he fully earned the generous applause he received.

This 18-year-old Gibraltarian, at present an RAF radar mechanic on National Service in Germany, seemed to have glue on his gloves as, time after time, he went high into the air to collar a ball from the wing meant for a Cardiff head.

5 APRIL 1958:

MIGHTY MACEDO – that's what everybody has been calling young Tony, and not everybody can be wrong. Tony's great keeping in recent weeks has thrilled hundreds of thousands of spectators, and now he is talked of as a future England goalkeeper. Undoubtedly he is one of the greatest keepers of his age this country has seen for many a day, and as we already know, his native Gibraltar is proud of him.

25 APRIL 1959:

It had to happen sooner or later, but all the same, our heartiest congratulations to our keeper Tony Macedo, upon his selection for the England Under-23 team to play the England team at Highbury, and then go to Italy to play the Italian Under-23 side in Milan on 10 May. From there the side goes to Bochum to play the German Under-23 side. Here's to some more great games, Tony!

commenced. This really was to be Fulham's year, and although there was some disappointment at the fact that Sheffield Wednesday pipped them to the Championship post (someone always seems to) the main aim of promotion to the First Division was achieved.

It had been a high-scoring season, and Tony only managed six clean sheets in 37 League appearances – but no-one was counting.

Fulham's re-introduction to First Division football did not go smoothly. Their young goalkeeper had remarkable talent, amazing agility and a good deal of self confidence, as well as excellent protection from George Cohen and Jimmy Langley, but he was unable to prevent Blackburn Rovers putting four past him on the first day of the season.

Fulham won four of the next six, but then travelled to Molineux. Confidence was high, the Cottagers having beaten Wolves 3-1 a week earlier, but Fulham were short of several key players and Wolves were ravenous for revenge. For all his cat-like prowling and his acrobatic leaps, Macedo was unable to prevent the home side from scoring nine times while his colleagues failed to reply.

Thus Tony Macedo held – and still holds – the record for the most goals conceded by a Fulham keeper in a League game. Things improved after that, however, and, although they later suffered a 5-0 defeat at home to Manchester United, three wins and a draw from their last four games saw Fulham finish in their highest ever League position – tenth in Division One. Tony had missed just three matches of the campaign.

Things got tougher in succeeding seasons, but Tony Macedo helped to keep Fulham in the First Division for another eight years. Little success came Fulham's way (unless one counts the annual Houdini impersonations) but there were some memorable encounters. Macedo would probably wish to forget a 7-2 defeat at Newcastle early in the 1960-61 campaign, as well as a 6-1 defeat at home to Sheffield United in January. In fact, he would probably wish to forget the entire season, as he missed a total of 13 games through injury. Yet his side still managed to finish 17th and lived to fight another season.

Tony missed fewer games in 1961-62 and, although the Cottagers narrowly avoided relegation, there was another good Cup run to savour. Victories over Hartlepools, Walsall (after a replay) and Port Vale led to a Sixth Round pairing with Blackburn.

After a 2-2 draw at the Cottage, at least one Fulham fan telephoned his employer to report sick as he waited outside the Golden Lion for the Supporters' Club coach which would transport him to Ewood Park. He later saw another excellent performance by Tony Macedo as Fulham won courtesy of a Maurice Cook goal.

Fulham were drawn against Burnley in the Semi-Final, and might well have beaten them. They took the lead through a Graham Leggat goal and, according to one press report, Jim Langley, playing the game of his life 'subdued the fumbling Burnley forwards to such a degree that Macedo was kept in idleness.' Unfortunately, Tony was later required to spring to life, but failed to stop an equaliser. Fulham lost the replay 2-1.

The 1961-62 season saw the start of Tony's longest injury-free period. He was ever-present in 1962-63, during which he registered ten clean sheets in the League, and had a consecutive run of four during March. Then he played in the first game of the 1963-64

COTTAGE COMMENT

12 SEPTEMBER 1959:
A shy boy of 15, obviously from 'furrin' parts, turned up at the Cottage one day and said he'd just left school and his teacher had sent him for a trial. That's how we got one of the greatest keepers in the business.

His name? Elio (Tony) Macedo, of course. Still 15 years of age, he played in our combination team and we said to ourselves: 'Wait till that lad's grown bigger and stronger. We've got one there!'

He had to wait nearly four years to get in our League side, and then, in his first match, we won 5-0. Some debut!

He's now played for the England Under-23 team, has played twice for the FA and was in the RAF Representative team when he did his National Service. Where will he go from there? All being well, quite a distance.

Born in Gibraltar, Tony was brought to England at three years of age, and then, four years later, was taken back again. He returned two years after that and went to school in north London, playing for his school, District and County. He is a keen cricketer, swimmer and badminton player, and hopes to be married just before Christmas.

MATCH ACTION

Writing in the *Daily Herald*, Peter Lorenzo had this to say about Tony's performance in the 1958 Semi-Final replay:
The new Red Devils have bounced through to Wembley, by courtesy of Tony Macedo the not-so-Magnificent...

This was the goalkeeper's 21st first-team game. No player has had a more bitter coming of age. In his other 20 senior outings the lithe, superbly built, superbly confident Macedo, fittingly tagged the Rock of Gibraltar, had never put a hand, a foot or even an eyelash wrong.

In his nightmare 90 minutes at misty Highbury yesterday the 'Rock' crumbled. Macedo, who looked the world's greatest on Saturday, became an ordinary mortal. He could be faulted for United's first goal. He literally gave away the second and third.

Fulham couldn't believe this was happening. Macedo, who had spurted past Chelsea's Jimmy Greaves as the south's Soccer Discovery of the Year, was in near tears as he lay beating the muddy turf with his gloved hands after his second major blunder in the closing seconds of the first half...

first two games of the 1966-67 campaign, but played for most of the rest of that season, Fulham finishing in an improved 18th position.

Opposite bottom: Tony claims a high ball against Nottingham Forest.

Even when Fulham lost heavily, Tony Macedo was often a hero. Following a game at Sheffield United in January 1967, which the Cottagers lost 4-0, part of a newspaper report read as follows:

'United, with only one win in the last ten matches, completed the double – and could have doubled their score. And if Macedo had not been in top form, they would have! Macedo repeatedly won admiration for keeping the score down, but Fulham were still lucky to get off so lightly. Their goal was almost constantly pummelled.'

The constant pummelling finally took its toll, and Fulham were relegated at the end of the 1967-68 season. Tony Macedo, plagued by injury, made only 18 League appearances, his last being in the penultimate game – a 2-2 draw at home to Southampton.

Early in the following season he joined Colchester United, initially on loan, and played 39 times for them before emigrating to South Africa, where he still lives. He was probably the best.

campaign, before suffering a knee injury. He was, however, back before Boxing Day and the visit of Ipswich. Tony conceded only a single goal in that game, but saw Roy Bailey of Ipswich let ten go by as Fulham romped to their record win.

In 1964-65, Tony missed only two League games as Fulham finished in 20th place. He missed more than half of the following season, having broken his jaw in a 4-1 home defeat by Northampton, but his side managed to finish 20th again anyway. Tony missed the

FULHAM RECORD

Seasons Played:	1957-68
Total Appearances:	391
Goals Conceded:	666
Average Per Match:	1.703
Clean Sheets:	73 (19%)
One Goal Conceded:	119 (30%)
Two or More Conceded:	199 (51%)
Most Conceded:	9 v Wolves, 16 Sep 1959, Div 1

JACK McCLELLAND

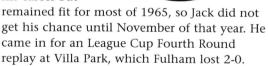

Jack McClelland was a goalkeeper unfortunate enough to spend a great deal of his time playing reserve-team football. Born in Lurgan in May 1940, he first joined Glenavon. He later moved to England and joined Arsenal where, between October 1960 and December 1964, he made 46 First Division appearances. Although signed as deputy to Jack Kelsey, McClelland still managed to win the first of his six Northern Ireland caps before he made his first-team debut for the Gunners. He went on to earn another five during his career, but continued to spend much of his time at Highbury playing in the reserves.

MATCH ACTION

Don McWhinnie wrote a newspaper report on a 2-2 draw at Liverpool in October 1966. It started like this:
Champions Liverpool must have thought they had been brought face to face with a combination of Batman and Superman.

Fulham's defence deserves credit for their magnificent second-half refusal to surrender. But the real giant of a man who repeatedly achieved the seemingly impossible was goalkeeper Jack McClelland.

It wasn't that Liverpool – having taken a lead in 50 seconds through Strong, fallen behind, and then reached equality – didn't shoot.

They rained shots at McClelland from every conceivable position in that after-the-interval onslaught. He stopped them all. Sometimes by luck. Sometimes by inspiration. But nobody can begrudge him his lucky moments.

Saves from Geoff Strong and Bobby Graham just didn't look on. Somehow the inspired McClelland got to them…

An unspectacular but very reliable goalkeeper, Jack joined Fulham in December 1964, this time as deputy to Tony Macedo. Tony was somewhat injury-prone towards the end of his career but remained fit for most of 1965, so Jack did not get his chance until November of that year. He came in for an League Cup Fourth Round replay at Villa Park, which Fulham lost 2-0.

With Macedo absent for much of the remainder of the season, Jack McClelland was to play a major part in Fulham's bid for First Division survival. The team was playing badly when he joined it, and the first four League games in which he featured were lost. On two occasions, at home to Burnley and at Leicester City, Jack conceded five goals, but then came the visit of his old club Arsenal. Fulham were beginning to look doomed to Second Division football, but Jack kept a clean sheet, the Cottagers won 1-0 and there was suddenly a glimmer of hope.

Macedo returned for the next two games (both resulting in 1-0 defeats – more doom and gloom) and then it was McClelland until the season's end. A goalless draw at home to Blackpool was followed by two more defeats, but then the revival began in earnest as Fulham won five on the trot, seven out of eight, and nine out of eleven. Highlights for

11 DECEMBER 1965:

With Macedo out manager Buckingham called on 25-year-old Irish international Jack McClelland – and so brought to an end an 11-month wait.

We signed Jack from Arsenal last Boxing Day but the consistency of Macedo has kept him away from his League debut for the club.

But patience is a strong virtue of McClelland, whose luck has been shoddy since he joined Arsenal from Glenavon.

After gaining a first-team place he broke his collarbone and struggled to win back a regular League spot at Highbury.

Nothing went right for him, and by the time Fulham came to sign him he was a very unhappy footballer. But he has found being an understudy to a consistent keeper like Macedo doesn't give much opportunity of first-team football. He stuck to it, however – and his reward came last week when newspaper headlines heralded the success of his comeback.

For a goalkeeper to come into League football and play so well after so long in the reserves is in itself a splendid feat. We wish Jack McClelland a long continuation of the great start he has made to his comeback.

Jack were no doubt a 2-0 win over Liverpool, a 3-0 win over Sunderland and a 1-0 win at Leeds (Fulham had lost the encounter at the Cottage four days earlier by three goals to one). Lowlights included a surprise 4-0 defeat at Craven Cottage by Leicester City, which threatened to halt the Great Escape.

A couple of 1-1 draws finished off the season and Jack, along with Steve Earle, Graham Leggat, Les Barrett, Bobby Robson and Johnny Haynes were heroes as Fulham finished in 20th place. This was not the end of Jack McClelland's Fulham career, but with Ian Seymour being brought in as Macedo's eventual replacement his appearances were limited. In 1966-67 he played just 11 first-team games, taking part in a 5-0 home win over Wolves in the League Cup in October and conceding six goals at Upton Park in November. During the following season he made just nine appearances and was between

the posts for the last game of the campaign, at Goodison Park. Fulham lost this one 5-1 but it mattered not as relegation, so long threatened, had finally been confirmed.

The 1968-69 Second Division campaign was to be Jack McClelland's last, and again he was to be involved in a unsuccessful battle against relegation. Having played in a handful of games in the earlier part of the season, he was loaned out to Lincoln City, but was recalled in March due to another goalkeeping crisis. He kept clean sheets at home to Millwall and away to Cardiff as Fulham won both games 2-0, but the Cottagers failed to win any of their last seven encounters and went down again. Jack's last match was at Selhurst Park, which Fulham lost 3-2.

McClelland was given a free transfer at the end of the disastrous 1968-69 season, and moved to non-League Barnet where he won an FA Trophy finalist's medal. He died tragically early in 1976.

Left: In action in front of the Cottage's largest crowd of 1964-65 – 36,291 v Manchester United.

FULHAM RECORD	
Seasons Played:	1965-69
Total Appearances:	57
Goals Conceded:	117
Average Per Match:	2.052
Clean Sheets:	11 (19%)
One Goal Conceded:	12 (21%)
Two or More Conceded:	34 (60%)
Most Conceded:	6 v West Ham Utd, 5 Nov 1966, Div 1

PETER MELLOR

For a goalkeeper who eventually came to be regarded by some as one of the best ever to play for Fulham, Peter Mellor made an unpromising start. Born in Prestbury in November 1947, he was an amateur with Manchester City and, even though he had won an England Youth cap, he moved to non-League football at Witton Albion when he was 20. Then came the first upturn in his career, when his services were purchased by Burnley for a small fee in April 1969. He was ever-present in Burnley's First Division side in 1969-70, making more than 50 League and Cup appearances, and it seemed his future was assured. But then things started to go wrong for him and the crowd at Turf Moor began to voice its discontent.

The Burnley fans were so vocal regarding Peter's performances that he decided he would

FIRST PERSON

I've been asked to write a few words about goalkeepers and it's been suggested that I knew Jack Fryer. This isn't true, although of course Alan Mullery remembers him well. I used to room with Alan, and he was always talking about him.

As for Peter Mellor, he was of course a great goalkeeper. Most players have a love-hate relationship with keepers as, at crucial times, they can win or lose a game for you. Peter was no exception; he certainly won the game for us at Carlisle in the Sixth Round in 1975, when we hardly got a kick until Les Barrett scored the only goal of the game.

Peter got us to that Cup Final and we always felt confident with him behind us. He was always very enthusiastic and he commanded the area. He intimidated the opposition. Sometimes he intimidated us too.

It's a little-known fact that Peter had funny fingers. Several of them had been broken, and so were crunched up in a sort of grip. This was why he would often palm the ball down before catching it, and was sometimes prone to punching the ball away.

Peter is coaching in Florida now, while I look after the Anguilla national side. I don't know too much about goalkeeping – I usually just tell them to sort of stand there and try to stop the ball going in – so I telephoned Peter and asked him to come down and show them how it's done. He was great. He wasn't at all intimidating…only half of them ran away!

My mum says he's the best goalkeeper Fulham ever had.

Les Strong

Peter Mellor was quoted as follows in a Fulham programme in March 1973:
The only place I didn't want to go to was London. I heard that house prices were dear and the people unfriendly. It was at the time of the power strike and my wife and I were sitting in darkness when Burnley manager Jimmy Anderson arrived to say a London club had made me an offer. Fulham.

As soon as I saw Fulham, I knew I'd made the right choice.

have to get away. He went on loan to Chesterfield for a month and in February 1972 Fulham, who were looking to replace Malcolm Webster, signed him for a fee of £20,000. Peter went straight into the first team.

Fulham were struggling to ensure continued Second Division status during the 1971-72 season, and Peter helped his new team to beat Bristol City 2-0 in his first game. This was just as well, as the Cottagers won only two of the remaining 12 games after that, and finished in 20th place. However, four of these matches resulted in goalless draws and there were no

rumblings of custodial discontent among the Fulham faithful. The blond bloke was doing very well.

Peter Mellor was ever-present in 1972-73 and Fulham's fortunes revived. With John Cutbush, Fred Callaghan, Paul Went, Jimmy Dunne and of course Alan Mullery to help him, Peter conceded just 49 League goals as Fulham finished ninth.

His goalkeeping style was perhaps a little eccentric, and he did sometimes punch the ball out when it looked easier to hold on to it, but everyone agreed he was doing an excellent job.

Injury cost Peter only four League appearances in the following season – and then came the 1974-75 campaign. This, of course, is the one remembered by every Fulham supporter who was to become a part of it. The League programme is largely forgotten, although Fulham, again finishing in ninth spot, had an excellent defensive record. Peter Mellor played in every game, and conceded just 39 goals in 42 matches. And, of course, he played in every FA Cup game.

The Cup run began with a tie against Hull City, which took three games to resolve. There were then four games against Nottingham Forest before the Cottagers emerged victorious to face Everton at Goodison Park.

FULHAM RECORD	
Seasons Played:	1971-77
Total Appearances:	224
Goals Conceded:	239
Average Per Match:	1.066
Clean Sheets:	80 (36%)
One Goal Conceded:	78 (35%)
Two or More Conceded:	66 (29%)
Most Conceded:	4 v Hull City, 11 Mar 1972, Div 2
	4 v Middlesbrough, 19 Mar 1974, Div 2
	4 v Plymouth Argyle, 27 Dec 1975, Div 2
	4 v Notts County, 17 Apr 1976, Div 2
	4 v Southampton, 2 Oct 1976, Div 2

The defence had conceded only six goals in the seven games prior to the Merseyside encounter, but few expected Fulham to progress further at the home of the League leaders – even with Peter Mellor in fine form. In the event Viv Busby scored twice and Peter, although almost causing members of the Fulham contingent to suffer cardiac arrest on several occasions, did his flamboyant stuff. Roger Kenyon had managed to put one past him, but Fulham were through to the Sixth Round.

The Cottagers were drawn away to Carlisle United. This certainly looked like a game which could be won, even though Carlisle were enjoying (well, perhaps not actually enjoying) their one and only First Division season. After the magnificent performance at Everton, there was a lot of interest in a Fulham side which contained Bobby Moore and Alan Mullery, and which was managed by the First Gentleman of Football, Alec Stock.

But Fulham had a hard time at Brunton Park, and were saved, quite literally, by a truly remarkable performance from Mellor. Peter dived, and leapt, and grabbed, punched the ball out and somehow kept the Carlisle forwards at bay. His opposite number, Alan Ross, had a pretty good game too, until he got in a tangle with one of his own defenders and allowed Les Barrett to score the only goal of the game.

Fulham had reached the Semi-Final stage for the fifth time, and on this occasion were due to go one stage further. It took two attempts before Birmingham were dispatched, and again it was Mellor, together with Moore and Mullery, who took the plaudits. After a 1-1 draw at Hillsborough, Birmingham were beaten 1-0 in extra time at Maine Road – and Peter was on his way to Wembley.

The Final against West Ham was a disappointment, not least for Peter Mellor, who was not at his magnificent best. Getting there had, however, been a tremendous achievement, and Peter would always be remembered for the part he played in the Great Cup Run.

It was back to the more mundane task of helping Fulham to a mid-table position the following season, and Peter played in every game, conceding only 14 times in home

League fixtures. In November 1976 he sustained a serious injury against Notts County, and this proved to be his final first-team appearance. He had a major disagreement with manager Bobby Campbell and, to the disappointment of many, left for Hereford United in September 1977.

Peter played 32 League games for Hereford before joining Portsmouth in July 1978. He enjoyed three good seasons at Fratton Park and appeared in 129 League encounters before retiring from the English game.

GERRY PEYTON

Gerry Peyton was, without doubt, another outstanding goalkeeper. He had the occasional off-day, of course, but as is the case with every good keeper, his mistakes were only memorable because of their comparative rarity. He is probably remembered less for his spectacular saves than for his many consistent performances, in which an excellent positional sense enabled him to stop very good shots from becoming very good goals.

Gerry was born in Birmingham in May 1956. He joined Aston Villa as a junior but was eventually rejected, later moving to non-League Atherstone where his fortunes improved considerably. Spotted by Burnley, he signed on at Turf Moor in May 1975 and later kept a clean sheet on his debut against Liverpool.

By December 1976, Gerry had lost his first-team place and, as had been the case with Peter Mellor in 1972, Burnley decided to do Fulham a favour by passing their spare goalkeeper on to the Cottage. The sum of £35,000 changed hands, and young Gerry arrived to spend the next ten years in London.

The new former Burnley goalkeeper replaced the older and now injured former Burnley goalkeeper and made his debut in a 5-0 Division Two victory over Oldham Athletic, in which George Best scored. Gerry naturally kept his place, and he also kept clean sheets in his next two matches. He then conceded a couple at Stamford Bridge and missed the next three games, before returning to the side to begin a run of 111 consecutive League and Cup appearances.

Fulham finished in 17th position in 1976-77 but, with Gerry ever present in the following season, managed a respectable tenth spot. They did the same in the following campaign, with Gerry missing just a couple of games through injury at the very end, but the highlight of 1978-79 was undoubtedly the Fourth Round FA Cup tie against Manchester United.

Left: Roger Brown looks on as Gerry Peyton thwarts Walsall, September 1980.

37

I was a Fulham apprentice when Gerry came to Craven Cottage, and I thought he was a great keeper. His shot-stopping was his finest attribute, and he used to bring off some brilliant saves.

He was also very, very brave. I remember the game at Middlesbrough in 1982 when he dived at the feet of Duncan Shearer and received a really horrific injury. He got up, holding the ball in one hand and his head in the other. When he let go of his head, blood spurted from it in a great fountain. The physio had to hold a large flap of Gerry's skin in place as he led him from the field.

Much later, Gerry came to West Ham for a short time, and I had reason to be very grateful to him. I was having a testimonial game and Gerry, in conjunction with Jack Charlton, got many members of the Eire squad to come to Upton Park. He was one of the best.

Tony Gale

Having disposed of Queens Park Rangers by two goals to nil (John Margerrison and Gordon Davies), the Fourth Round game drew over 25,000 to the Cottage on a freezing Wednesday evening. It was a fiercely competitive encounter, but Gerry acquitted himself magnificently. Jimmy Greenhoff scored with the aid of the woodwork against the run of play, but John Margerrison equalised and Gerry and his pacemakers prepared for the replay at Old Trafford.

There was to be no repeat of the 1974-75 Cup run, as United won the replay by a single goal but much worse was to follow for Bobby Campbell's Fulham side. In October 1979 Gerry, by now a regular in the Eire side, was injured in a domestic game against Notts County (strangely, the same fixture in which Peter Mellor had been injured three years earlier) and Perry Digweed took over for seven matches. Gerry returned, but was unable to prevent his side from slipping down the table and finishing the season with relegation to the Third Division. The Cottagers failed to bounce straight back and, at the end of December 1980, Gerry temporarily lost his place to the emerging Jim Stannard, but he was back for the start of the following season – which was to be a great deal more fun.

The 1981-82 campaign began with a 2-1 defeat at home to Brentford, but things soon improved and, with Gerry back at his best, Fulham began to climb the table. A run of four mid-season clean sheets and other excellent performances by Gerry helped the Cottagers challenge for promotion back to Division Two. Everything rested on the last home game, with Fulham needing a draw to go up, while the visitors, Lincoln City, needed to win to achieve the same happy ending for themselves. It was a nerve-jangling evening for manager Malcolm Macdonald and the 20,000 fans but, though Gerry did let one past him near the end, a Roger Brown header was enough to send the vast majority home in transports of delight.

A run in the League Cup, culminating in a Fourth Round defeat by a single goal at White Hart Lane, had also added spice to the 1981-82 season, but 1982-83 was to be even more exciting, although ultimately terribly disappointing. Gerry Peyton was ever-present

Gerry Peyton writes from Kobe, Japan:

I have been coaching Vissel Kobe for almost four years now and last season we won promotion to the J League – a kind of Japanese Premiership. It has all been a lot of fun and very good experience and I've enjoyed every minute of it.

Things were a little tricky at the start, though. For one thing, not long after I signed my contract, there was a terrible earthquake which caused devastation across a wide area. Fortunately, I was in Los Angeles visiting my daughter at the time and I could hardly believe what had happened to the city when I returned.

I have no regrets about retiring from the English game a little early. After Fulham and Bournemouth, I deputised at Everton and West Ham – and at one or two other clubs – and when the coaching opportunity came up I grabbed it with both hands (cue Les Strong joke about it being the first time I grabbed

anything with both hands). My only regret is that the revival of Fulham Football Club did not happen while I was still at the Cottage.

I have so many happy memories of Fulham. Alec Stock was a true gentleman and I also remember the late, great Bobby Moore with affection. I can remember Tommy Trinder and, if I try really hard, I can even remember Strongy. In those days the Cottage housed the players' bar and there was a warm feeling about the place. If only money had been spent on the team at the right time, Fulham might now have been in the top flight.

However, it seems that the top flight beckons once more. I was delighted when I heard that Mr Al Fayed was putting money into the club and I wish Kevin and Ray, and everyone connected with Fulham, all the very best in the future. I shall continue to watch out for the results, as I always do, and when I get back to England my first port of call will be Craven Cottage.

in a campaign which, with just five games to play, had seen the Fulham defence concede only 40 goals in 37 League encounters. (Actually, Gerry was not quite ever-present – he needed 23 stitches in his head following an injury early in a tremendous 4-1 victory at Middlesbrough in September, and was forced to hand over his jersey to Kevin Lock. Being Gerry, however, he was back in the side for the next game.)

Fulham, having looked certainties for promotion and likely Division Two Championship contenders, lost four of the last five games – including the game at Derby which was brought to an early end by appalling behaviour on the part of a large number of County supporters – and failed to go up. It was a great opportunity lost, and Gerry was as devastated as the rest of the Fulham squad.

Opposite: Peyton exerts a calming influence.

Left: In action against Bristol Rovers, April 1982.

In a Fulham programme from February 1979, Gerry Peyton is profiled as follows:
Since coming to the Cottage in December 1976, Gerry's brave and acrobatic displays have established him as a firm favourite with the crowd. Last season he was our only ever-present and his performances have not gone unrecognised by the international selectors.

He was called up by Don Revie to join the England Under-21 side in 1976-77 but Gerry, although born in Birmingham, chose to play for the Republic of Ireland, his parents' birthplace. He made his international debut in February 1977 when he came on as substitute against Spain in Dublin, and since then he has won three more caps, against Bulgaria, Turkey and Poland.

Although Gerry has played in almost 150 first-class matches, and won international honours, he is still only 22 years old and looks set to make the goalkeeping position his own for many years to come.

GERRY PEYTON TESTIMONIAL
FULHAM v CHELSEA
WEDNESDAY, 7th MAY 1986 KICK-OFF 7.30 p.m.
SOUVENIR PROGRAMME PRICE 80p

Thus began one of the darker periods in Fulham's history. The next two seasons saw the Cottagers achieve mid-table positions, with Gerry going on loan to Southend for a short period but otherwise sharing Fulham first-team duties with Jim Stannard. Gerry had the lion's share and although Jim had played in the first League Cup encounter with Liverpool in November 1983, it was Gerry who was chosen for the first and second replays. As usual, he played well and shared in the disappointment when the Reds finally won the tie by a single goal at the Cottage.

With Stannard moving to Southend during 1985, Gerry embarked upon his final season at Craven Cottage. It proved to be a miserable League campaign, relieved only by two League Cup games against Chelsea. Gerry did well, but the replay at the Cottage was lost on penalties. Fulham once more lost four of their last five League games, and the result was 22nd position and relegation to Division Three.

Gerry had had enough of Fulham. His record had been an excellent one, but a testimonial game was the only reward for his ten-year stint, after which he was allowed to leave for Bournemouth even though his international career was not quite over. Gerry spent several happy seasons at Dean Court, making more than 200 League appearances, before ending his playing career as a journeyman keeper with a number of clubs – including Everton and West Ham.

FULHAM RECORD	
Seasons Played:	1976-86
Total Appearances:	395
Goals Conceded:	501
Average Per Match:	1.268
Clean Sheets:	100 (25%)
One Goal Conceded:	156 (40%)
Two or More Conceded:	139 (35%)
Most Conceded:	5 v Swindon Town, 11 Jan 1977, FAC
	5 v Wolves, 19 Feb 1977, Div 2
	5 v Burnley, 18 Nov 1978, Div 2
	5 v Hull City, 9 Nov 1985, Div 2

ARTHUR REYNOLDS

Fulham used four goalkeepers during the 1909-10 season and, when Arthur Reynolds made his debut in the penultimate Division Two game, few would have realised that they were witnessing the start of an incredible 15-year career at the Cottage.

Arthur played his first match on 23 April 1910, a 2-2 draw at Lincoln, his last appearance being at home to Clapton Orient (a 2-0 defeat) on 18 April 1925. In-between times he featured in a total of 399 League encounters, 21 FA Cup games and 42 First World War fixtures – more games than any other Fulham goalkeeper.

Arthur Reynolds was born in June 1889 and started with his home-town club, Dartford. During the four seasons he spent there, he helped his side to win Dartford League and Kent League titles, and then Phil Kelso (the manager who later helped Fulham avoid a merger with Arsenal, God bless him) signed him for the Cottagers. Leslie Skene and

Jack Fryer were at the end of their careers at Fulham, and 20-year-old Arthur soon found himself playing in the Football League. He was ever present for the next two seasons and missed only two matches during 1912-13.

Fulham were very much a mid-table team during almost all of Reynolds' career, finishing tenth, eighth, ninth, 11th and 12th in the seasons immediately preceding the war. Although they had a number of fine players in the side, including wing-half Jimmy Torrance and goalscoring centre-half Fred Mavin, things would probably have been a great deal worse had Arthur not been between the posts.

In his first full season, Reynolds kept nine clean sheets, and followed this up with another nine in the 1911-12 campaign, and eight in 1912-13. Results for Fulham fans to savour included a 1-0 win over Chelsea in December 1910, and a very nice 3-0 beating of Liverpool (the first ever encounter between the two clubs) in the FA Cup Second Round in February 1912.

There was the occasional hiccup, notably a 4-3 defeat at home to Burnley in October 1911, which was followed a week later by Derby County ramming home a round half-dozen to beat Fulham 6-1. Apart, however, from a home game against Bradford in February 1914, this was the only occasion in which Arthur conceded more than five in a League match.

Reynolds missed a few games due to injury in the last two pre-war seasons, but continued to astonish the assembled populace when he was playing by displaying a remarkable degree of agility and invention. Most goalkeepers prefer to use their hands when making saves, but Arthur was happy to use any part of his body available at the time, and in consequence it was no surprise to see a foot, a forearm or even a knee employed in the art of shot-stopping.

Many keepers do use their legs, but often this is from necessity rather than choice. In Arthur Reynolds' case, his legs were an essential part of his armoury and he employed them to marvellous effect.

The Great War eventually caused a cessation of League hostilities, but it was no great surprise when Arthur returned to duty on a regular basis early in the first postwar season. Not much had changed, except that Fulham finished the 1919-20 campaign in a slightly higher than usual sixth place.

FULHAM RECORD	
Seasons Played:	1909-15 and 1919-25
Total Appearances:	420
Goals Conceded:	503
Average Per Match:	1.197
Clean Sheets:	141 (34%)
One Goal Conceded:	140 (33%)
Two or More Conceded:	139 (33%)
Most Conceded:	6 v Derby County, 4 Nov 1911, Div 2
	6 v Bradford PA, 21 Feb 1914, Div 2

COTTAGE COMMENT

From Cottage Chronicles – An Anecdotal History of Fulham Football Club (1994):
Arthur Reynolds holds a number of records. From March to October 1920 he went nine home games without conceding a goal, and kept six clean sheets on the trot in the League in seasons 1921-22 and 1922-23.

Arthur played in 127 consecutive League and Cup games from May 1921 to March 1923.

**WOLVES 2 FULHAM 1
(19 OCTOBER 1912):**
There was a remarkable incident in the first half: Reynolds, in trying to clear, punched at the ball and in doing so dealt Charlton a severe blow in the face. The game had to be stopped while the right-back was attended to.

**FULHAM 1 COVENTRY CITY 0
(11 OCTOBER 1919):**
Fulham's last line of defence won them the points, Reynolds being on top of his form. He punched away corner after corner that Coventry gained in rapid succession, and stopped, and scooped out shots in wonderful fashion.

**CARDIFF CITY 3 FULHAM 0
(9 OCTOBER 1920):**
Fulham were not in their best form, though Reynolds may be commiserated with on being beaten three times after a magnificent display.

His clearances were delightfully clean and accurate throughout, and he had plenty of chances of distinguishing himself because of the weakness of the men in front of him.

**FULHAM 5 BIRMINGHAM 0
(25 MARCH 1921):**
Fulham were thorough in their methods, and no-one did better than Reynolds. This goalkeeper never made anything like a mistake, and it is due to the losers to write that they were clever enough to compel some of the very best of goalkeeping in order to avoid a score.

**FULHAM 1 BLACKPOOL 0
(20 SEPTEMBER 1924):**
Fulham had most to thank Reynolds, who made a couple of sensational saves, from Barrass – the brainiest forward on the field – and Mee, the fastest, when Blackpool were in full sail.

Arthur had represented his side whenever he could throughout the war years, and continued to make his presence felt by missing only seven games in the next five seasons – being ever-present in 1921-22 and 1922-23. During those two seasons he had a run of five, and then a run of six games in which the opposition failed to score, and he managed another nap hand of clean sheets in 1923-24.

Fulham occupied the Second Division throughout Reynolds' entire career, but even though Ernie Beecham took over from him after the 1924-25 season, the team struggled for a number of years in Arthur's absence. His influence had been enormous as, apart from anything else, his voice could be heard for miles.

There is no doubt that he was a great goalkeeper, and yet he won no international honours and his sole excursion into the higher reaches of the game came in October 1914 when he played in a representative match for the Football League against the Southern League.

It might have been different had he moved to First Division Blackburn, when Rovers tried to purchase his services just before the war, but Arthur remained at the Cottage to become another Fulham legend.

Arthur Reynolds moved to Clapton Orient in 1925, but played only a couple of reserve-team matches before retiring from the game. He continued to support Fulham, however, attending many fixtures at the Cottage until his death on 14 March 1970.

Sadly, the passing of one of their greatest goalkeepers went officially unremarked by the club. One can only assume they were not informed since, just two weeks after Arthur's passing, the programme printed an obituary for former assistant manager Joe Edelston. Celebrated by many for his presence between the posts for so many years, Reynolds was, for the first time, conspicuous by his absence.

IAN SEYMOUR

Ian Seymour had all the makings of an excellent goalkeeper but his first-team chances were severely restricted, firstly by Tony Macedo and secondly by serious injury. Born in Edenbridge in March 1948, he was signed by Fulham from Tonbridge in August 1966. Macedo was injury-prone and coming towards the end of his career and, although Jack McClelland was also on the books, it seemed that Seymour was, in all probability, the man of the future.

Ian, at times a spectacular keeper capable of making some quite remarkable saves, did not have to wait too long to make his debut. It came at Old Trafford in March 1967 and the critics had nothing but praise for his efforts. Macedo came back after that match, however, and another chance did not come until the second game of the 1967-68 season. This proved to be a 3-0 defeat by Sunderland at Roker Park, but Ian kept his place for the next five matches before being replaced by McClelland.

FULHAM RECORD	
Seasons Played:	1966-71
Total Appearances:	75
Goals Conceded:	120
Average Per Match:	1.600
Clean Sheets:	16 (21%)
One Goal Conceded:	25 (34%)
Two or More Conceded:	34 (45%)
Most Conceded:	5 v Arsenal, 28 Oct 1967, Div 1
	5 v Manchester City, 16 Mar 1968, Div 1
	5 v Charlton Ath, 30 Nov 1968, Div 2
	5 v Cardiff City, 7 Dec 1968, Div 2

Two League encounters and one League Cup game later, Ian was back in the side for five First Division defeats (culminating in a 5-3 scoreline at Highbury) – a run which was only slightly ameliorated by a 2-2 draw at Workington in the League Cup, followed by a 6-2 victory in the replay. Macedo then came back from injury once more and played until February before hobbling off in favour of Ian again. This time Seymour had a run of just four games, keeping a clean sheet in the first – a rare 2-0 victory (over Sheffield Wednesday) during that relegation season – but conceding five at Maine Road. Ian played only one more

Ian was only just 19 when he played his first League game for us and, of all places, it was at Old Trafford. We lost 2-1 but I remember thinking how well he played, especially for a goalkeeper with so little experience.

Ian was not with us long enough to prove just how good a goalkeeper he might have become, because his career was cut short by injury. He certainly impressed everybody in his first few games, and we were all very sad when he eventually had to give up.

Les Barrett, one of Fulham's finest postwar wingers

League game during that campaign (his side going down 3-0 at Old Trafford) as Fulham sunk into the Second.

The following season was another disastrous one for Fulham, which ended in relegation for a second successive season. It wasn't too good for Ian Seymour either. Macedo had come to the end of his time at the Cottage, so Ian started the 1968-69 campaign as hopeful as everyone else that the side would bounce straight back. With Seymour between the posts, the first game resulted in a 1-0 win over Bristol City, but after that it was downhill virtually all the way – the next two matches being drawn and the following four all resulting in defeats.

Fulham's main problem at this time was an almost total inability to score: Ian conceded only eight times in the first nine games, after which he shared the goalkeeping duties with McClelland until Brian Williamson arrived on the scene in December.

Seymour played under four managers during his relatively brief career at Craven Cottage. Vic Buckingham was succeeded by Bobby Robson, who briefly passed the poisoned chalice to Johnny Haynes, before it ended in the hands of Bill Dodgin Junior.

This must have been most unsettling for everyone, and may help

to explain why Ian occasionally appeared to lose concentration and make the simplest of goalkeeping errors. Over the next two seasons he shared first-team duties with Malcolm Webster and, with Fulham doing quite well in Division Three, put in some excellent performances. One can only imagine his delight at seeing Steve Earle score five in the historic eight-goal trouncing of Halifax in September 1969.

Although the duties were shared with Webster, the former Arsenal keeper had the lion's share, and Ian's first-team days were almost over. In 1970, while playing for the reserves in a London Challenge Cup game against Enfield, he broke his leg diving bravely at an attacker's feet. The damage done during this encounter eventually forced him to give up the game, his last League match being a 4-1 defeat at the Vetch Field in December 1970.

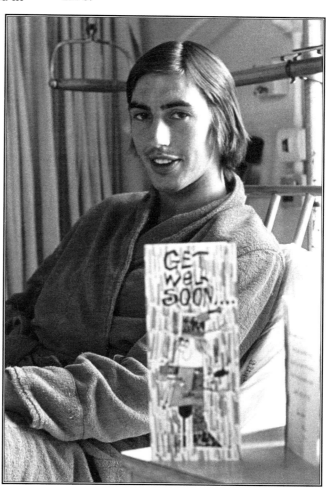

The Fulham programme had this to say about Seymour's debut:

The Fulham debut of Ian Seymour, 19-year-old goalkeeper from the Kent village of Edenbridge, came suddenly and dramatically. Ian had nearly got his first-team chance when Tony Macedo couldn't play in the FA Cup tie against Sheffield United. Jack McClelland was chosen instead. Ian said then: 'I'm disappointed, but my chance will come.'

It did – on Tuesday and in the dream setting of Old Trafford against United in our return Easter match.

Any fears manager Vic Buckingham had about subjecting Ian to the atmosphere of an Old Trafford packed with 51,000 were soon dispelled. Ian made two great saves early on and according to one reporter has 'tremendous composure and very sound judgment'.

It was our old friend Nobby Stiles who finally beat Ian after 70 minutes with a glancing header. But Steve Earle, coming on as substitute for Mark Pearson, gave us an equaliser.

Ian's chance of sharing in a creditable draw was sadly spoilt when, with only 40 seconds to go, Bill Foulkes snatched a winner with a header.

Ian will certainly be much better for the experience. He has certainly come a long way since we paid just over £1,000 for him from Southern League Tonbridge. Considering he has played only 14 games in the Football Combination, his progress has been remarkable.

Ian was a young giant when he arrived at Fulham. Harry Haslam had got him over from Tonbridge, and he was a quiet country lad who took his goalkeeping very seriously. He was very shy. He used to slip in and out of the dressing room almost unnoticed and he was not one to accompany the other lads when we all disappeared in the direction of the Kings Road after training.

Ian and I got on extremely well until a game at Newcastle in 1967. I was playing at centre-half and at one stage I lobbed the ball back to Ian. Unfortunately I didn't lob it well enough and Albert Bennett, the Newcastle centre-forward, nipped in, inadvertently kicked Ian in the head and scored. Ian needed six stitches and was *ever* so pleased with me.

I believe Ian Seymour could have been a great goalkeeper. I remember him sustaining a number of injuries, including broken fingers, and I know he was devastated when a badly broken leg ended his career.

John Ryan, who played for Fulham between 1965 and 1969

Left: Ian keeps his eye on the ball while the Riverside Terrace watch the 1968 Boat Race. The match, a friendly against Kilmarnock, was won 3-1.

LESLIE SKENE

Born in August 1882, Leslie Skene first became interested in goalkeeping while studying to be a doctor at Edinburgh University. He played a little for Stenhousemuir before moving to Queen's Park in 1901, where he won a Scottish international cap, conceding one goal in a draw with Wales in 1904.

One assumes that Leslie Henderson Skene tired of life as an amateur in his native land, and therefore decided to abandon the vast acres of Hampden Park in favour of the big time at Craven Cottage. At any rate, he was persuaded to move south in 1907 in time for Fulham's first match as a Football League side, and he remained a Fulham player for three seasons.

The 1907-08 campaign proved to be an eventful one for the Cottagers. If they hoped their new international signing, brought in as a replacement for the badly injured Jack Fryer, would help them to become established as a League side to be reckoned with, then their hopes were more or less justified.

Fulham lost the opening game 1-0 at home to Hull City, but Leslie kept the first of his 24 clean sheets in the next match at Derby County, which Fulham won by the game's only goal. The next match saw Fulham beat Lincoln City 6-1 before an estimated 20,000 crowd, and this was followed by a 1-0 home defeat by Grimsby.

MATCH ACTION

**Extract from a match report –
Derby County v Fulham (Football League Division Two) played on 24 April 1909.
Fulham lost 2-1.**
The second half was all in favour of Derby County, who were nearly always attacking and gave Skene a tremendous amount of work to do.

He had shots from all sorts of positions but he was never at a loss to deal with them, and the only occasion on which he was beaten the referee gave Garry offside. He had a great reception from the crowd, which he richly deserved.

Leslie had therefore made a more than competent start, conceding just three goals in his first four outings, although as he journeyed south from Barnsley on 28 September he probably wished he had not stopped off in Yorkshire but had carried on back to Scotland. Barnsley had put six past him, and the Cottagers had failed to reply.

So the new goalkeeper, described as having 'keen vision, sure hands and pluck' was far from infallible. Fulham were, however, to finish fourth in the Second Division table at the end of that first League season.

Much of the credit must go to the relatively diminutive Skene (he stood at just five feet eight and a half inches) although the rest of the Fulham defence, which included Harry Ross, Pat Collins, Billy Morrison and Billy Goldie from the Southern League days, must not be forgotten.

On 11 January 1908, Fulham travelled to Luton for a First Round FA Cup game. Luton had lost their place in the Football League in 1900, and were not to regain it until 1921, but they still managed to place the ball in Leslie's net on three occasions during that game.

No matter, Fulham scored eight and moved on to the next round. Norwich and Manchester City (after a replay) were the Cottagers' next victims, with Leslie conceding just three goals in the three games. And then came the visit of all-conquering Manchester United to London SW6.

Sadly, the Red Devils were mighty even then, and were to win the First Division title that season. But they were to prove no match for fearless Fulham. A crowd of 41,000 saw Fred Harrison score twice for the home side, and also saw Leslie Skene make two excellent first-half saves to keep Fulham in the game. United did manage to pull one back in the second period, but it was the London side which went into the hat for the Semi-Final draw.

Poor old Les. He was forced to take some of the blame as Fulham crashed 6-0 to Newcastle in the Semi-Final three weeks later, but at least he helped his club to achieve their best ever run in the FA Cup.

The next two seasons (1908-09 and 1909-10) saw Fulham finish in tenth and seventh position in Division Two, with Leslie making 52 further appearances – Jack Fryer mainly taking over in his absence until the advent of Arthur Reynolds towards the end of the 1909-10 season.

Leslie Skene left Fulham in 1910, and transferred himself to Glentoran. No fee was payable as he had left the Football League, which was a pity because Fulham were hard up in those days. Dr Skene later moved to the Isle of Man to become a medical officer at a mental hospital.

FULHAM RECORD

Seasons Played:	1907-10
Total Appearances:	94
Goals Conceded:	123
Average Per Match:	1.308
Clean Sheets:	24 (26%)
One Goal Conceded:	38 (40%)
Two or More Conceded:	32 (34%)
Most Conceded:	6 v Barnsley, 28 Sep 1907, Div 2
	6 v Stoke, 21 Dec 1907, Div 2
	6 v Newcastle Utd, 28 Mar 1908, FAC

JIM STANNARD

Jim Stannard was born in London in October 1962. He played for Ford United before joining Fulham, signing professional forms in June 1980. Gerry Peyton was very much Fulham's principal goalkeeper at the time, and Perry Digweed was still about, so naturally it was junior-team football for the 17-year-old Stannard.

He did extremely well in the juniors, but hardly expected to be drafted into the first team less than four months after his 18th birthday. His chance did, however, come at the end of January 1981. Fulham were doing badly in Division Three and had won just two of their previous 21 League games. Gerry had been having something of a rough time and Malcolm Macdonald decided to give Jim a game in a friendly against Brighton. He then asked him to make his League debut at home to Swindon.

Few of the dispirited supporters watching this game can have realised that they were witnessing the first appearance of a goalkeeper who was, in time, to become a cult figure at the Cottage. Spirits were, however, raised by his, and Fulham's, performance, as the Cottagers won 2-0 and Jim kept the first of his many clean sheets.

Jim did not actually have a great deal to do in that game, but he certainly did well enough to hold his place for the rest of that improving season. He went on to make another 16 appearances and to keep another five clean sheets, as Fulham rose to an almost respectable 13th place in the table.

Gerry Peyton returned to the side at the start of the 1981-82 promotion campaign,

Left: Stannard gets plastered! Jim takes it easy after breaking his leg in late 1979. He sustained the injury while still a young apprentice behind Peyton and Digweed.

Jim is an excellent keeper, and a real character. He may have given the management a few minor problems during his time at Fulham and yes, he could occasionally be a bit reckless, but he gave some memorable performances.

I've worked with a number of top goalkeepers and I can honestly say that Jim was a rival to them all. I saw him make some quite unbelievable saves during his Fulham days and could never quite work out how such a big man could move in the way that he did.

Of course, there were two Jims – the one who saved Fulham from defeat on numerous occasions, and the one who thought he was an outfield player! I remember a game at Mansfield, played in dreadful conditions, where we were holding on quite well. Then Ronnie Mauge played the ball back and Jim thought he could beat the Mansfield forward to it. Unfortunately he couldn't, and Mansfield went one up. We were trying to sign Simon Morgan at the time and he was watching that game with me. After Simon had seen Jim make that little error of judgment, it took him about six months to decide to join Fulham!

Jim also had a few problems with crosses, but there's no doubt in my mind that over the years he did a great job at the Cottage and fully deserved the praise and admiration of the Fulham fans.

Ray Lewington

and kept young Jim out of the team for all but two games. Jim was sidelined again the following season as Fulham tried desperately to gain First Division status. He was still a young keeper and accepted reserve-team football happily enough, especially as Gerry gave him a lot of help and encouragement, but must have wondered when his chance would come again.

It came at the start of 1983-84. Jim played in the first 15 League games and also featured in two 3-1 League Cup victories over Doncaster and a tremendous 1-1 draw at home to Liverpool in the same competition. Gerry had, somewhat surprisingly, gone on

loan to Southend, but to Jim's dismay was recalled in time for the second and third games against Liverpool. He was back in the reserves again.

In September 1984, Stannard also went on loan to Southend. He returned to the Cottage for a few mid-season games and was then loaned to Charlton in February 1985. A few weeks later he journeyed once more to Roots Hall, and was officially transferred on deadline day by Ray Harford, for a fee of £12,000. Was this the end of Jim Stannard's career at the Cottage? It was not.

Jim's last League game before his transfer to Southend had been at a windswept Fratton

Park, where he had played quite well in the second half. Unfortunately, he had conceded four goals in the first period of this quite remarkable game. Dean Coney, Leroy Rosenior, Gary Barnett and Kevin Lock had eventually secured a rare 4-4 draw, but few who saw that game were surprised when Stannard left the club shortly afterwards. The surprises came later.

Jim came into his own while at Roots Hall. Named as first-choice goalkeeper, he did not miss a game and helped his side win promotion from the Fourth Division. With Gerry Peyton having left for Bournemouth a year earlier, Jim returned to the Cottage in the summer of 1987. The deal was brokered by Jack Burkett, and by the time he returned Stannard was a very accomplished keeper.

Fulham beat Colchester United 3-1 in the Littlewoods Cup in the first game of the 1987-88 season, after which Jim kept five clean sheets in six games. The Cottagers finished their Division Three campaign in ninth place and Jim, the only player to be ever-present, made a total of 53 appearances (including two in the Freight Rover Trophy).

Fulham made the play-offs the following season, with Stannard missing just one game on the way. Jim was by now becoming something of a legend, his substantial build belying his speed of movement and capacity for instant reaction.

He was actually being recognised as one of football's finest shot-stoppers and, importantly, the supporters loved him dearly. Even so, 1988-89 saw a few difficult

Below: The goal Jim may have scored at Crewe in September 1989. Some say it made contact with Andy Sayer on the way – but Jim says it didn't!

Lilliewhite interviewed Jim for a series in the 1990-91 Fulham programme entitled 'The Best and Worst of...'

Here is an extract:

'Sorry I can't give you a best save,' Jim apologised. 'The thing is, being six foot two and 15 stone, I'm a big boy to get past and I'm able to produce reflex saves, many of which I could count as "bests". I enjoyed that 45 minutes against Everton at the start of the season, for example, and thought it would take something a bit special to beat me that night. In fact, McDonald's penalty kick did the trick but that was unstoppable.'

Talking of penalties, I asked Jim if he'd ever thought of volunteering to take one. He laughed. 'The gaffer says we're at the point where he'll start with me and work right through the team until he finds someone who can score...'

At this point Mark Newson arrived with a couple of toasted cheese sandwiches which was Jim's lunch getting cold. So I sat back in a pleasant reverie with thoughts of him smacking penalty kicks past all and sundry.

'The best grounds I've played at have got to be St James' Park, Newcastle, and Maine Road, and one of the worst is Northampton*. I can't blame the pitch there for probably the worst goal I've ever conceded, though. A long cross, two or three years ago, and I lost it completely; it slipped right through my hands and straight in – and a 3-2 defeat was the outcome.

'On the other hand, I remember playing a blinder at Bramall Lane on one occasion. We still lost by a single goal, but everything came to hand. The trouble is, when you do well you're often told that's what you're paid for; one mistake and you're in the dirt – literally.'

* Jim was alluding to a game at the Recreation Ground: Northampton had yet to move to Sixfields. There, before the start of an evening game in November 1994, the lower part of Jim suddenly disappeared from view. A large hole, caused by the previous insertion of rugby posts and some very wet weather, suddenly became much larger and Jim started to sink.

The start of the game was delayed for 20 minutes while little men with little buckets of sand tried desperately to fill the hole. The match did eventually get under way, Fulham became the first visiting team to win at Sixfields – and Jim kept a clean sheet.

encounters. The Cottagers lost 5-2 at Molineux, but were possibly buoyed by the fact that without Jim it would have been far worse, and were certainly heartened by the sight of Gordon Davies breaking Johnny Haynes' goalscoring record.

But can anyone explain how Fulham, having won 4-1 at Preston a few days earlier, then went down 7-0 at Chester on 5 April? In fact, this was partly due to the fact that Jim was carrying an injury, but even so it was a shock.

The play-off games against Bristol Rovers also proved a disappointment, and Jim prepared for another season in the Third Division – one which was to see the Cottagers narrowly avoid relegation to the basement division, and which, incidentally, saw the reserves finish bottom of the Football Combination. Poor overall team performances notwithstanding, Jim Stannard kept 13 clean sheets in 1989-90, and played in all but two first-team games. The 1990-91 campaign was as bad for Fulham, with relegation only just avoided once more. Jim missed a handful of matches but was still playing very well and many supporters continued to be surprised that he remained at Craven Cottage rather than going on to better things.

The 1991-92 campaign was a better one for Fulham, even though Alan Dicks was still in charge of things at the start. A place in the play-offs was not quite achieved, but Jim kept 18 clean sheets in the League and main Cup competitions and had a run of six in Division Three matches between 28 February at Wigan and 20 March, at home to Hartlepool. The next season saw Fulham mainly occupying mid-table positions while Jim, naturally, was guarding the goalmouth.

Before the start of the 1993-94 season, Division Three was conveniently renamed

FULHAM RECORD

Seasons Played:	1980-82, 1983-85 and 1987-95
Total Appearances:	430
Goals Conceded:	593
Average Per Match:	1.379
Clean Sheets:	115 (27%)
One Goal Conceded:	147 (34%)
Two or More Conceded:	168 (39%)
Most Conceded:	7 v Chester City, 5 Apr 1989, Div 3

Division Two, thus ensuring that, when they were relegated at the end of the campaign, Fulham would not find themselves in the Fourth. Unlucky Jim was doomed to be ever-present for the third time in his Fulham career as the Cottagers suffered their most disastrous campaign up until that time. It all started well enough with a 1-0 victory at Hartlepool, but Fulham failed to win any of their next five League games and proceeded to slide rapidly down the table.

Jim's confidence can hardly have been heightened by young Mr Fowler's five goals in the League Cup game at Liverpool, and less than a month later he conceded six at Exeter City. When asked about that ridiculous 6-4 defeat, sometime manager Ray Lewington replied 'Don't ask. It was just one of those games.'

Jim had done his best in the last match of the season at the Vetch Field, but Fulham were down. He remained at the Cottage until the end of the next season, once more playing in the majority of first-team games, before moving to Gillingham following a dispute over his contract. He had played a vast number of games for Fulham, as well as quite a few for Southend, and he went on to create records in his first season at the Priestfield Stadium.

While helping his new club to promotion from Division Three he kept 29 clean sheets – a club record – and conceded only six League goals at home, and 20 in all – a new Division Three record. He also won the PFA Divisional Goalkeeping Award once more, having previously won it while at Southend.

As he indicates in his introduction to this book, Jim Stannard never wanted to leave Fulham. He was undoubtedly one of the club's greatest assets and almost certainly saved the side from earlier relegation. It's a pity that Fulham Football Club chose to ignore this in the summer of 1995.

Below: Jim flies through the air with the greatest of ease at Gigg Lane, Bury, in April 1991.

ALF TOOTILL

Known as 'The Birdcatcher',
Alf Tootill was relatively
small by goalkeeping
standards, but he made up
for his lack of inches by the
possession of a safe pair of hands and
lightning reflexes. Born in Ramsbottom in
November 1908, he was an excellent cricketer
and played for his local Lancashire League
side. As a goalkeeper he joined his local Bury
Amateur League team, and then moved on to
Accrington Stanley. He had not been long
with Third Division Accrington when, in
1929, he was spotted by Wolverhampton
Wanderers of Division Two and was signed for
a £400 fee.

Alf continued to play cricket and in 1930
he topped the batting and bowling averages
for his side. He also established himself in the
Wolves team and played in every League game

FIRST PERSON

I remember Alf Tootill as a not very tall but
very active goalkeeper. I think they used to
call him 'The Birdcatcher' but, as a ten-year-
old, I somehow always associated him with
Tootal ties, which were famous at the time.
Tootill was playing in the replay versus
Chelsea in 1936, and I had escaped from
school as usual.

Fulham seemed to have the game sewn
up, and although Tootill let in a couple near
the end, I seem to remember he had a pretty
good game. Basically, I think he was
probably a good goalkeeper playing in what
was, most of the time, a fairly ordinary side.

**Arthur Vincent, who used to bunk off
school in the 1930s to watch Fulham's
midweek games**

COTTAGE COMMENT

**In the *Cottagers' Journal* – the programme
for a game against West Ham on
7 November 1936 – this appeared,
following a 2-0 defeat at Leicester:**
The rather serious injury to Mike Keeping
was a big handicap to our side...

Under the circumstances it would be
hardly fair to criticise our players but Tootill,
Birch, Gibbons, Tompkins and Hammond
made many commendable efforts in their
fight against the odds.

**The writer of these lines was obviously
keen to leave no defender or star player
unpraised, but it seems to have worked.
Alf kept a clean sheet in the West Ham
game, and Fulham scored five.**

in their 1931-32 Second Division Championship campaign, conceding just 49 goals in 42 matches. In all, he made 143 League and Cup appearances for Wolves, but found life a little harder when his side reached the top division. Fulham signed him in November 1932, having bizarrely called him out of a Wolverhampton cinema in order to obtain his signature.

Fulham were going well in Division Two. Having recently been promoted back to this level, they were looking for their own version of the double – promotion in two consecutive seasons – and Tootill went almost straight into the side. His first game was at the Valley, where he took part in a victory by the odd goal in three, but he then saw his team slip into a familiar mid-season run of poor performances which, in the end, cost them that hoped-for second promotion. Alf's next ten games in fact produced two wins, two draws and six defeats – including a 5-0 FA Cup defeat at Third Division (North) Chester. Jake Iceton then returned to the side for four games before Alf came back for the last 13, during which Fulham rose to a final third place in the table.

The 1933-34 season saw Fulham have something of a difficult time. They finished in 16th place but, all things considered, their

defensive record was not too bad. Alf conceded 68 goals in his 42 League and FA Cup appearances. In the following season, with his side finishing seventh, he was ever-present and conceded 59 in 43 games.

In League terms, 1935-36 was fairly

ever Cup match against the old enemy.

A total of 50,000 people witnessed the tie and, although the ball entered the net on more than one occasion, the game finished 0-0. Chelsea had one strike disallowed for offside in the first minute but Alf came into his own shortly afterwards when he saved a close-range drive seemingly destined for the back of the net. Fulham were three up in the replay at the Cottage a few days later, but the defence seems to have lost concentration towards the end of the game and Alf was given something of a hard time. Chelsea scored twice near the finish, but the Cottagers went through.

Life was a lot easier in the Sixth Round game against Derby County. While Johnny Arnold, Albert Barrett and Trevor Smith were knocking them in at the other end, the Fulham keeper probably had time to reflect on how far he had come since his Ramsbottom days. His reverie was briefly interrupted during the second half when he was obliged to make a brilliant one-handed save, but that was about it until his side visited Alf's old home, Molineux, for the Semi-Final against Sheffield United.

The game was a disappointment as Fulham went down 2-1 and, although he had played well and could not be faulted for either goal, Alf's dreams of FA Cup glory faded forever. He again missed only one match during the following season, but Fulham signed Hugh Turner and Alf effectively became Hugh's deputy at the start of the 1937-38 campaign. Alf's last League match for Fulham was on New Year's Day in 1938, a 3-2 defeat at Plymouth Argyle, and he left the Cottage for Crystal Palace in the summer of that year.

Shortly before Alf Tootill left for Crystal Palace, this appeared in a newspaper: 'Fulham keepers, Tootill and Turner, are both Lancastrians. Tootill comes from Bury and Turner from Wigan. Before the ban dropped on unrestricted transfers, there was a chance that Tootill would return to Lancashire. Blackburn Rovers were interested. I believe they made a definite offer. Negotiations were halted when Tootill got a groin injury.'

Alf Tootill played only one League game for Palace, but made a number of wartime appearances at Selhurst Park. He died in 1975.

ordinary for Fulham (ninth) and for Alf Tootill. He missed only one match, conceded six goals at Newcastle and five at Leicester – but stood and watched his team beat Nottingham Forest 6-0 and both Bury and Port Vale 7-0. Moderately exciting stuff, but it was in the FA Cup that the action really occurred. After Third and Fourth Round victories over Brighton and Blackpool, Fulham marched over to Stamford Bridge for their first

FULHAM RECORD	
Seasons Played:	1932-38
Total Appearances:	214
Goals Conceded:	306
Average Per Match:	1.429
Clean Sheets:	56 (26%)
One Goal Conceded:	71 (33%)
Two or More Conceded:	87 (41%)
Most Conceded:	6 v Newcastle Utd, 28 Sep 1935, Div 2

HUGH TURNER

Noted for his agility and anticipation, Hugh Turner was another of the smaller goalkeepers who made an impression at Craven Cottage. He was, rather unforgivably, born in Wigan in August 1904, but his parents did the decent thing and moved to a village near Gateshead shortly after his second birthday. Hugh first played for Felling Colliery in Darlington in 1924 (his father having been a miner) and then moved to High Fell of the Northern Alliance before joining Huddersfield Town not long afterwards.

Hugh gave sterling service at Leeds Road throughout the late 1920s and early 1930s. He played for England against both France and Belgium in May 1931, and during the same year represented the Football League against the Irish League. These were exciting times for Huddersfield who, having won the League Championship three times in a row between 1924 and 1926, were seldom far from the top of the table during Hugh's early years with the club.

FIRST PERSON

Peter Carrie, a Plymouth Argyle supporter who came to Craven Cottage with his father in the 1930s and 1940s, remembers a match in April 1939:
Fulham were playing Blackburn Rovers and I can still see Dusty Miller breaking down the left wing, chasing into the penalty area and pushing the ball across the goal for Dennis Higgins to score from close range. Ronnie Rooke made it 2-0 not long afterwards. Fulham eventually lost that game 3-2 and I imagine that Hugh Turner, whom I remember as a very good goalkeeper, was not amused at the result.

Hugh Turner gained an FA Cup runner's-up medal in 1930 when his side were gunned down 2-0 by Arsenal, and in all made almost 400 League and Cup appearances for the Terriers. He fell out of favour in the 1936-37 season, whereupon he journeyed south to the Cottage to become the replacement for Alf Tootill.

If Hugh thought that by dropping down a division he would have an easier time, then he had another think coming. He conceded four goals in his first game on the opening day of the 1937-38 season at Plymouth Argyle, and another nine in the next five matches. Tootill then returned to the side, but Fulham's Second Division fortunes failed to improve and, in January 1938, Hugh came back and was ever-present until the war interrupted all proceedings a season and a half later.

The Cottagers did rather well towards the end of the 1937-38 season. Young Joe Bacuzzi

Seasons Played:	1937-39
Total Appearances:	71
Goals Conceded:	93
Average Per Match:	1.309
Clean Sheets:	22 (31%)
One Goal Conceded:	23 (32%)
Two or More Conceded:	87 (37%)
Most Conceded:	5 v Sheffield Wed, 27 Dec 1938, Div 2

and not so young Mike Keeping were maintaining tight security at the back while Ronnie Rooke was knocking them in at the other end. Fulham won seven of the last eight League games (Hugh proving that he was still unhappy playing on the south coast by conceding four at Southampton to mess up the sequence) with Ronnie scoring hat-tricks in the last two games – a 4-0 home win over Bury and a 3-1 victory over Blackburn, also at the Cottage. Fulham finished eighth and Hugh Turner had kept eight clean sheets in 26 League outings.

Hugh played in every League and FA Cup game in the last season before the outbreak of global hostilities. It was not a particularly spectacular campaign in terms of results, although the first three matches were won and in two of them Hugh maintained total security. There was too a remarkable encounter at the Cottage in October, when Millwall were the visitors and a record number of 49,335 fans attended to see (if they could)

A newspaper report on a game played on 12 March 1938:

TURNER ALONE STARS FOR FULHAM
Manchester United 1 Fulham 0
This result bears little resemblance to the state of the game at Old Trafford, where Fulham were practically run to a standstill. The score might have approached double figures in United's favour if their forwards had been able to shoot well.

They hurried when they had time to take their aim. They got the lead in the seventh minute when Baird netted the ball after Turner had advanced following clever work on the right wing by Smith. But they should have been at least three goals ahead at half time.

Turner gave a superb display of goalkeeping. His methodical timing of his punches and advances to meet centres and shots earned the full ovation the crowd gave him as he left the field.

In the second half, United missed two chances in the first five minutes and four minutes later Dennison was carried off through injury to the left knee. He did not return.

Rowley, who recovered from a trip, cut in and scored into the far corner of the net with a low shot. Then, to the crowd's astonishment, the referee disallowed the point and gave a free-kick to United.

what turned out to be a very exciting game. Hugh conceded an own goal by Mike Keeping in the first half, but Fulham went on to win 2-1 with strikes from Viv Woodward and James Evans.

By the season's end, Hugh had conceded 55 times in 42 League games as the Cottagers finished 12th and waited for war. He also kept a clean sheet in an FA Cup game at home to Bury, while Rooke scored all six goals for Fulham. The Cottagers had experienced some strange results against Bury over the years but perhaps the strangest was yet to come, as in the first postwar League match the men from Gigg Lane were to put seven past the Fulham keeper. By this time, however, Hugh's playing days were over.

The 1939-40 season had only just begun when it was abandoned due to the outbreak of a greater conflict, and Hugh returned north to find work in the engineering field. His wife had been distraught at the news of his transfer to Fulham in 1937, but the couple had settled in well and now Mrs Turner was sorry to leave.

Much later, she told Huddersfield Town's club historian that she missed the teas, laid out on a cloth-covered billiard table in the Cottage, which were provided by the club for the players' wives. She had also enjoyed sitting on the Cottage balcony to watch the game.

In 1949 Hugh Turner became the first coach of Huddersfield's youth team, in the newly formed Northern Intermediate League. He eventually retired from coaching but maintained a lifelong connection with Huddersfield Town Football Club. There may have been no teas laid out on a billiard table at Leeds Road, but Huddersfield is a friendly club and is always keen to welcome old players.

Accordingly, Hugh eventually became a fervent supporter of his first League side and could be seen and heard cheering on the Terriers at home games throughout the 1960s and into the 1990s. He became too frail to attend matches and died early in 1997 at the age of 92, just a few weeks before he was due to be interviewed for this book.

Hugh Turner did a very good job at Fulham, and although he was transferred by Huddersfield in the 1930s, he is now a legend at the club where he first established himself as a fine goalkeeper.

MALCOLM WEBSTER

This section ends with a goalkeeper who was much maligned during his time at Craven Cottage. It is therefore somewhat surprising to note that, despite a period during which he seemed able to do nothing right, his overall record is actually rather a good one.

Born in Rossington, Yorkshire in November 1950, Malcolm was an apprentice at Highbury. He won England Youth honours but made just three League appearances for the Gunners, where he was understudy to Bob Wilson. He came on loan to Fulham in December 1969, went straight into the League side and stayed there until the season's end. In May 1970 he was officially transferred to the Cottagers for a £10,000 fee.

The 1969-70 campaign was Fulham's first in the Third Division. They were to finish in fourth place and, a season later, were to win promotion back to the Second. Malcolm's debut was a 3-1 home win over Bristol Rovers and the 19-year-old keeper largely impressed. During his 26 appearances in 1969-70 he let in just 25 goals, helped by an improving defence and the fact that Fulham were, after all, now in Division Three.

Bill Dodgin Junior had no hesitation in forking out the relatively modest fee when the time came to settle with Arsenal, and Malcolm duly continued to show that it was money well spent. Fulham won seven of their eight opening League and League Cup games in

1970-71, and Malcolm kept clean sheets in five of them. In all, he played in 38 games during the course of that season, conceding only 29 goals.

Had Malcolm Webster carried on in that vein, his record would have been better than that of almost any other Fulham goalkeeper. With promotion back to Division Two however, someone altered the script and it has to be admitted that Malcolm had more than the odd poor game.

The 1971-72 campaign started well enough for him with a clean sheet at home to Watford, but after that things went a little awry. He conceded four apiece at Swindon and Sheffield Wednesday before Portsmouth put half a dozen past him in a dreadful 6-3 defeat at Fratton Park.

Fulham won their next four games after that particular humiliation, but even so there was only one clean sheet for Malcolm and in February 1972 he lost his place to Peter Mellor.

For the rest of that season, and all through the next, Mellor made the Fulham goalmouth his home and Malcolm failed to get a look-in. The latter played reserve-team football until 31 October 1973 when, with Mellor injured, he began a run of six consecutive first-team games. The last of these, a 2-0 defeat at West Bromwich Albion, proved to be his farewell.

Malcolm moved to Southend United in January 1974, made more than a hundred appearances for them, and then went on to Cambridge in September 1976. He was still not yet 26 years old and his goalkeeping days were far from over.

FIRST PERSON

From an interview with Malcolm Webster in the Fulham programme in March 1971:
As the spectators know, I like to let the other defenders know what's going on behind them so they don't need to turn round. I'm told they call me the Sergeant Major, but I don't mind. I used to get a few comments from behind the goal when I was at Arsenal and I let it bother me for a while.

It's different at Fulham. At any rate, if they say anything I don't hear them. What I've learned is that you can only do your best. Nobody can expect more of you.

FULHAM RECORD	
Seasons Played:	1969-72 and 1973-74
Total Appearances:	104
Goals Conceded:	128
Average Per Match:	1.230
Clean Sheets:	32 (31%)
One Goal Conceded:	38 (36%)
Two or More Conceded:	34 (33%)
Most Conceded:	6 v Portsmouth, 23 Oct 1971, Div 2

Success returned to Malcolm Webster at the Abbey Stadium, as he won a Fourth Division Championship medal in his first season, helping Cambridge to promotion to Division Two a season later.

His playing career ended in 1984 but he is still involved with football. If you listen carefully you may just be able to hear one of the loudest voices in football barking out instructions to the goalkeepers of Ipswich, where he currently coaches.

THEY ALSO SERVED

Every young player, when joining a major football club, has high hopes of glory. Yet only a few go on to achieve stardom and many never make the grade. Some, while never to become a Johnny Haynes or an Alan Shearer, manage to at least make a living from the game.

An outfield player who has ability and determination will, if he perseveres, probably get into the first team and stand a fair chance of keeping his place – there are, after all, quite a few defenders and midfield players in a side, as well as a couple of strikers, and most footballers are reasonably adaptable. It's different for goalkeepers. There can only ever be one at a time and if a club has a particularly good one, it is very hard for anyone else to break on to the scene.

This section deals mainly with the Fulham keepers who never quite managed to establish themselves as first-team regulars, or who did not last very long when they did. It may have been because they weren't quite good enough, they were prone to injury, or because they happened to be around while someone else was stealing the show.

1898-1939

The first of these goalkeepers is **ALBERT MAILE**. Albert was with Fulham in the Second Division of the London League, and was keeping goal when his side beat Harrow Athletic 13-0 in January 1898. He was Fulham's first-choice keeper when the Reds, as they were then known, entered Division Two

of the Southern League later that year. He featured in all but two of the 22 League games during that 1898-99 season, and was also between the posts when Fulham beat the 2nd Coldstream Guards (4-0) and the 3rd Grenadiers (8-1) before going down 1-0 to Hammersmith Albion in the Third Qualifying Round of the FA Amateur Cup. Albert rather unfortunately conceded 41 League goals, and Fulham finished two places off the bottom of the table.

Albert Maile played in only four Southern League games in 1899-1900 plus a First Qualifying Round FA Cup match against Queens Park Rangers, which Fulham lost 3-0. During the season, his place was taken by **JACK HEAD**, who helped his side to a much more respectable second place and the chance to qualify for Southern League Division One status. There was, however, a hurdle to overcome in the shape of a test match and Jack, his brows corrugated in concentration, succumbed five times to the steely determination of Thames Ironworks while his team-mates could manage only one strike in reply.

Head missed only one game the following season, Fulham finishing fifth in the table, but there was more humiliation at the feet of QPR in the FA Cup – Jack suffering even more than his predecessor as Fulham crashed out 7-0. Fulham won the Southern League Division Two title in 1901-02, with Jack almost ever-present but again lost the test match, this time 3-1 to Swindon Town.

By 1902-03 the Southern League seems to have been falling apart as there were only six clubs left in Division Two. Fulham was one of them, but decided also to re-join the London League so there would be more games to play. Head played in all ten Southern League matches that season but Fulham also enjoyed a bit of a Cup run. They were only qualifying rounds, but Jack kept five clean sheets in seven games before his side finally went down 5-1 at Luton.

Fulham had, perhaps unsurprisingly, won the Second Division title again. Equally unsurprisingly, they had lost the test match (7-2 to Brentford). This should have proved a disaster for the Cottagers, but luck was on their side and the hammering counted for nothing as Fulham were allowed into the Southern League First Division anyway. On reflection, the Brentford game probably did count for something, as Fulham were told they had to raise a 'first-class team' by the end of May. Among many other players, they signed a goalkeeper called Jack Fryer – and that spelt the end of Head's Fulham career.

Fryer helped Fulham to gain Football League status by 1907-08, whereupon Leslie Skene took over as first-choice keeper. During

the 1909-10 season however, Fulham used four goalkeepers in their Division Two side – and **WILF NIXON** was not one of them. Jack and Leslie were coming to the end of their respective Fulham careers, Rudolph O'Donnell was playing his three matches on loan from Reading and Arthur Reynolds was just getting started. Wilf is reputed to have signed during 1909, but there was no place for him in the team until Reynolds missed a couple of games late in 1912.

Nixon was born in Gateshead in October 1882. He played for Wallsend Park Villa and Newburn FC prior to signing on at the Cottage. With Fulham now playing in the Football League, competition for places was a little tougher than it had been – and Wilf was no spring chicken. It seems he may have been economical with the truth when asked to provide details of his date of birth (either that, or the programme got it wrong – surely not?) but at all events his 30th birthday was behind him when he finally made his first-team debut in a 2-1 defeat at Bristol City on Christmas Day 1912. Fulham travelled to Leeds City three

Opposite: Albert Maile.

Top: Chairman Ernie Clay presents Wilf Nixon, 97, with a club history book in 1979.

days later, and Wilf went with them, playing his part in a 3-2 victory. He took no further part in League proceedings until 21 November 1914, when he kept a clean sheet in a game at Leicester Fosse, this being followed by his Cottage debut – a 2-0 win over Barnsley.

The Great War was by now well under way, but Wilf's priorities were beating the likes of Stockport County and Glossop North End rather than the Hun and he played in a total of 21 League and FA Cup matches that season. Nobody considered the possibility of the war lasting very long – but it did, and League Football was suspended for the duration at the end of 1914-15.

Arthur Reynolds was in goal for many of Fulham's wartime matches in the London Combination, but Nixon played in the first four games when League football resumed in 1919. He did well in the first two, as Fulham beat South Shields 1-0 at home and Clapton Orient by the same margin away, but two defeats and five conceded goals later, Arthur was back. Wilf was to play in only two more first-team games for Fulham, in the 1920-21 season, before calling it a day at the age of 38.

Nixon had keen eyes and a safe pair of hands, and was due to live for a very long time. Having visited Craven Cottage to celebrate his 100th birthday, he finally died in April 1985 at the age of 102.

One less appearance for Fulham's first team, and **TOM McKENNA** would not have made it into this section of the book – although in view of his rather unfortunate record he would probably not have minded too much! Tom hailed from Stewarton in Ayrshire and came into this world in September 1900. He played for Dalry Thistle before joining Fulham and arrived at the Cottage at a time of change on the goalkeeping front. The long career of Arthur Reynolds was drawing to a close, while Ernie Beecham was yet to make his debut.

MATCH ACTION

Extract from a newspaper report on Tom McKenna's last match for Fulham (17 October 1925), a 2-0 defeat by Clapton Orient:

Sympathies were with Fulham because they were handicapped by the injury of their goalkeeper, the direct outcome of which was that Orient took the lead in the 25th minute. Until then they had less of the play than the home team.

McKenna was in a collision with Cock, whose elbow caught him a blow in the face, and knocked him out completely. He continued to hold the fort until the interval, but obviously he knew very little about what was happening, and in the second half Chaplin went into goal. McKenna returned sometime after the game had been restarted, and wandered about the field in a semi-dazed condition.

The mishap occurred in front of the Fulham goal, and the referee had no option but to throw the ball down. The usual scramble followed, and for a moment the home defenders looked like clearing, but the ball cannoned back to the feet of Hannaford, who shot into the corner of the net.

It seems that, in 1925, an elbow in the face was regarded as a 'mishap'…

MATCH ACTION

This was how one reporter covered a game against Brighton played on 26 April 1930, which Fulham won 5-1 and which saw Bill Mason as the Cottagers' goalkeeper:

Brighton gave a feeble display. The result rather flattered Fulham, who were, however, decidedly the stronger side.

Hammond, Haley and Price were the outstanding figures among the home forwards and it was fitting that they should share the goals, three of which were credited to Hammond.

There was a 'scene' after Hammond scored the second. Brighton claimed that the ball had been handled and one of the linesmen waved his flag, but the referee refused to listen to the protests, or to consult the linesman.

There was some delay in restarting the game, and some of the Brighton players were so aggressive that it would have been no surprise had 'marching orders' been given.

Vallance and Kirkwood (who was Brighton's scorer) had several hot shots well saved by Mason, who also stopped a penalty-kick taken by Dutton.

McKenna's own debut came towards the end of the 1924-25 season, one week after Reynolds' last game. The result was a 2-1 victory at Crystal Palace, and this was followed by a 1-1 draw at home to Port Vale. Tom must have spent a happy summer contemplating a full Second Division campaign, but his hopes were to be dashed.

Len Boot donned the gloves for the first three games of 1925-26, let in eight goals and gave Tom the opportunity to establish himself. But Tom then conceded four at Oldham and, though he partially redeemed himself with a clean sheet in the next game, he then let in six, four and five against Swansea, Chelsea and South Shields respectively. The Fulham defence was in disarray, with only Reg Dyer, Len Oliver and Albert Barrett making more than 30 appearances during the course of the season, but it was evident that McKenna was not the man to stand behind them, and he played only three more times – sustaining an injury in his last match, against Clapton Orient in October. He left for South Shields in August 1926 and later played for Charlton Athletic, Merthyr Town (where he was player-manager), Southend United and Portadown.

Born in Earlsfield on 31 October 1908, **BILL MASON** was playing for Isthmian League Wimbledon when he was persuaded to join Fulham in September 1928. He came to the Cottage as a strongly built and muscular amateur, but manager Joe Bradshaw talked him into turning professional when first-choice Beecham suffered a serious injury.

Bill made his League debut on 10 November in a 2-0 defeat at Brighton, but he kept his place for the rest of the season (except for one game, when his near-namesake Meeson took over) and helped his newly relegated side to a modest fifth place in the Third Division (South). During this period he kept six clean sheets, but conceded five goals on two occasions. Beecham returned to duty at the start of the 1929-30 campaign, and Mason was restricted to a mere seven League appearances. By the beginning of the following season Jake Iceton had come on the scene, and from then on Bill was restricted to reserve-team football.

This was probably a pity, as Mason's performances after he left Fulham rather suggested that he should have been given more of a chance at the Cottage. He helped the reserves to second place in their table in 1932-33 and then moved to QPR, where he played 245 League and wartime games. When the war was over and his professional playing days were done, Bill decided to become Old Bill and joined the force, later keeping goal for Wimbledon Police and 'B' Division. He died in Bognor Regis in 1995.

Opposite: Tom McKenna.

Top: Bill Mason, whose career encompassed three London clubs.

Born in Hyde during October 1919, **MARK RADCLIFFE** played 88 games for Oldham Athletic during the war, before signing for Fulham around the start of the 1946-47 season. He was tall and well built and, having done quite well at Boundary Park, he probably hoped and expected to become a regular in the League side. This was not to be, as Fulham had a surfeit of goalkeepers at the time and the competition for places proved to be intense.

MATCH ACTION

This is from a newspaper report on Fulham's 2-0 defeat at Leicester City in the first postwar season. The season was an incredibly long one, and this game was played on 7 June 1947.

FINE GOALKEEPING BY RADCLIFFE
Fulham had the best of matters territorially, Shepherd being conspicuous on the left wing. From one of his efforts, Bradley had to run out of goal and fist away.

Leicester came more into the picture and Radcliffe, the Fulham goalkeeper, brought off more remarkable saves, notably one from Adam which he turned round the post for a fruitless corner. Radcliffe also made exceptionally good saves from Lee and Griffiths.

Attacks on both Leicester wings saw a terrific struggle in the Fulham goalmouth, where Radcliffe saved from all the Leicester forwards...

Oswald Evans played in the first game of the season (details of poor Ossie's dramatic League debut appear elsewhere in this book) and then Ted Hinton took over until the advent of Doug Flack. Radcliffe played first-team football on only 13 occasions during the two seasons he spent at Craven Cottage, but he did get a run of nine consecutive outings between December 1946 and March 1947. Fulham were struggling in the Second Division when Mark arrived on the scene, and they continued to do so during those nine games, losing five (including an FA Cup Third Round tie at Birmingham) and drawing one.

Mark kept only one clean sheet in his 13 appearances (a 2-0 home win over Bury) and disappeared from view at the end of the 1947-48 season, following just one League game during that campaign and an FA Cup Sixth Round appearance at Blackpool, which Fulham lost 2-0. He played one game for Rochdale in 1952.

Had it not been for a riot at the ground of Belfast Celtic in March 1949, neither Johnny Campbell nor Robin Lawler would have become Fulham players. And neither would **HUGH KELLY**. All three were signed when the Northern Ireland club folded after the riot and, although Lawler is easily the best-remembered, the other two each made a contribution at the Cottage.

Born in August 1914, Hugh joined Belfast Celtic during World War II and won two Irish Cup winner's medals as well as Irish League representative honours. He was kept out of Fulham's Second Division Championship side by Doug Flack and, towards the end of the season, by Larry Gage, but he finally made his debut in Fulham's first Division One season – at home to Chelsea on 17 September 1949. According to one press report, this was not the most inspiring of debuts:

'Fulham need a better working arrangement between backs and goalkeeper. Once more, against Chelsea yesterday, they gave away a goal through a stupid misunderstanding. I blame Hugh Kelly, the Irishman playing in the League side for the first time, for an error of judgment that led to this goal.'

Nevertheless, Fulham earned a rare point from this encounter with the Blues, and Hugh kept his place for a few more games before Doug Flack returned to the side.

Hugh Kelly was to remain for only one season at Craven Cottage, and was then swapped for Ian Black of Southampton. Kelly made just 27 appearances in a Fulham shirt, but while in the first team was called up for international duty by Northern Ireland. He was to make three more appearances for his country before the end of his career – one of which, while he was still a Fulham player, resulted in a goalless draw with Wales. The first of them, however, against England at Maine Road, ended in disaster. Arthur Rowley's brother Jack scored four times for England as the Northern Irish went down 9-2.

Hugh Kelly made 28 League appearances for Southampton and another 99 for Exeter City, before retiring in 1955. He died in 1977.

COTTAGE COMMENT

This was how the Fulham programme welcomed Frank Elliott in March 1954:
To fill the gap in the ranks of our goalkeepers caused by the injury to Ian Black, we signed Frank Elliott from Stoke City just before the 'deadline' last Tuesday.

Frank, who is a native of Croydon, had two seasons with Swansea before joining Stoke, for whom he played in Division One and Division Two. He will be remembered for his brilliant display on our ground early this season.

Ian Black's injury left us without an experienced goalkeeper, a situation which was aggravated by the fact that it was never certain that Brian Ronson, who is doing his National Service, could be released by the Army to play for us every Saturday.

The Fulham programme seldom gets anything wrong (!) so the fact that **FRANK ELLIOTT** was listed as 'a native of Croydon' in 1954 when he seems to have been born on 23 July 1929 in Merthyr Tydfil must have been due to some strange geographical aberration on the part of the editor. Whatever Frank's origins, he joined the Cottagers in 1954, more in hope than expectation of a regular first-team place. He was a temporary replacement for Ian Black, who had broken his arm, but Frank made a solid start, keeping a clean sheet in a 3-0 home victory over Bury in March.

In the remaining seven games of the 1953-54 season he conceded 16 goals but he was between the posts again at the start of 1954-55, playing in the first 11 matches. Ian Black then returned, and Frank was to feature on only seven more occasions.

Somewhat surprisingly for a 'native of Croydon', Frank had won a Welsh Cup winner's medal in his early days as a Merthyr Tydfil player, and had moved on to Swansea and then Stoke, before joining Fulham. On leaving the Cottage in 1956 he signed for Mansfield, for whom he went on to make 63 League appearances.

Opposite: Hugh Kelly, Fulham's second international goalkeeper.

Top: Frank Elliott, who notched 26 appearances in a Fulham shirt.

KEN HEWKINS who, as far as anyone knows, never went to Croydon or Merthyr Tydfil, was a native of South Africa. He was signed from Clyde in November 1955, during another injury crisis, and proceeded to become Fulham's most injury-prone goalkeeper himself!

Born just three months later than Elliott, Ken first became a goalkeeper at the age of 12 – because he was taller than most of his friends – and found he enjoyed it. A year later he joined a team in the Transvaal League, keeping goal in a side otherwise made up of 16 year olds. He then joined a team called Germiston Collies (no wonder he was later dogged by injury) and was spotted by a former Aberdeen player who was scouting for Clyde in South Africa. He signed professional on the spot, and in July 1949 arrived in Scotland.

Ken enjoyed some success with Clyde. He was brave and fearless, and in 1955 won a Scottish Cup winner's medal, keeping a clean sheet against Celtic. His first appearance for Second Division Fulham resulted in a 2-1 victory at Stoke City, and this was followed by a similar win at home to Plymouth. So far, so good, but then followed a trip to Anfield and defeat by seven goals to nil. This resulted in Frank Elliott's recall to the side, but two defeats later (the second being a 6-1 thrashing

at Lincoln which turned out to be Elliott's last game) and Ian Black was back from injury. Ken played just three more first-team games that season and with Black back he only featured on five occasions in 1956-57.

As understudy to Black and, later, to Tony Macedo, Hewkins played a lot of reserve-team football. He was the reserves' penalty taker, and had a very fierce shot. He was, in fact, a far better goalkeeper than his record suggests and, had his bravery not caused him so much injury trouble, he may well have qualified as one of Fulham's finest keepers. A severe ankle injury finally forced his retirement following four appearances in the 1961-62 season – all of which resulted in First Division defeats for Fulham. Ken returned to South Africa, where he still lives.

MATCH ACTION

From a report in the *News Chronicle* on a 1-1 draw at Blackburn on 5 October 1957:
HEWKINS IS GREAT
Hewkins played a blinder and when Rovers were pressing for a winner, his anticipation and fearless courage saved a hatful of goals...

The second half was a breakneck marathon. But as Blackburn piled on pressure, Fulham faded. A long Clayton throw-in nearly produced the winner. Cairns, thirty yards out, first timed a perfect drive.

It is a long time since I saw a finer shot – or a finer save. Hewkins soared upwards and sideways and fingertipped the ball from his goal.

Born in March 1928, **DAVE UNDERWOOD** had already made 223 League appearances before he was signed by Fulham manager Bedford Jezzard in 1963. Beddy needed an experienced keeper to cover for Tony Macedo's enforced absences, and Dave was to play in a total of 16 further League encounters during the 1963-64 season.

Dave's varied career had seen him play for Queens Park Rangers (Division Two), Watford (Division Three South), Liverpool (Divisions One and Two) and Watford again in Division Three (South) and in Division Three. He had also played for Dartford in-between times. At the age of 35 he clearly relished the chance to try his hands once more in the First Division, and he did well enough, keeping a clean sheet against Sheffield Wednesday on his Fulham debut.

This was followed by a 2-1 victory over Birmingham and a couple of 3-0 away defeats after which, Dave having played several games with a broken toe (for which the programme said he should have been awarded a 'soccer badge of courage'), Beddy was forced to draft in young Martin Townsend.

Poor Martin let in eight during those two games, and Dave was back in the side, dodgy toe notwithstanding. The team was struggling to score goals at this stage but George Cohen and Jim Langley, together with Alan Mullery, were keeping things pretty tight at the back. Only ten League goals were conceded during Dave's second spell between the posts, in a total of 11 games.

Tony Macedo returned from injury towards the end of November and Dave took part in only one more first-team game that season – a 3-0 defeat at Old Trafford. Tony remained almost injury-free during 1964-65, and Underwood had only three opportunities to shine, all within a seven-day period. The first encounter was at Nottingham Forest on 19 September, which Fulham won 3-2, the second was on the Wednesday, when they beat Oxford United 2-0 in the League Cup, and the third was on the following Saturday when they went down 4-1 at home to Stoke City.

That was it as far as Dave Underwood's Fulham career was concerned, although he went on to play for Dunstable, Dartford (again) and later managed Hastings United.

During the 1970s he became chairman of Barnet and later went to live in South Africa, where he died in 1989.

By the start of the 1968-69 season, Fulham Football Club was in crisis. Having struggled to remain in the top division for a number of seasons the Great Drop had finally occurred, and the Cottagers found themselves back in Division Two. The club itself professed optimism – older supporters will remember that in the first programme of the new season a little notice appeared stating that: 'We decided not to fly the flags of Second Division clubs this season. We didn't think it worth buying a set for just one season!'

Oh dear, how unfortunate. The First Division flags, which had fluttered so bravely and proudly by the side of the Thames, were furled and put away for ever – while the Cottagers proved the programme writer absolutely correct, and were duly relegated for the second successive season.

BRIAN WILLIAMSON was signed during that awful campaign. Born in October 1939, Brian had begun his professional career with Gateshead, who lost their League status in 1960. He moved to Crewe Alexandra, where he helped his side beat

Opposite: Ken Hewkins.

Top: A never before seen shot of Brian Williamson at Portsmouth, 1969.

Chelsea in an FA Cup game at Stamford Bridge and then, in December 1962, to Leeds United, where he was understudy to Gary Sprake. After only five League appearances with the Elland Road outfit, he moved to Nottingham Forest in February 1966. At Forest he was deputy to Peter Grummitt, but he did play in the League side on 19 occasions (as well as playing half a dozen games for Leicester City on loan) before moving to Fulham in December 1968 for a £10,000 fee.

When he joined Fulham, Brian naturally expected more first-team football, but with Ian Seymour (frequently injured, but still around), Jack McClelland and, a little later, Malcolm Webster on the books, his chances proved to be limited. He made his Fulham debut in December 1968 in a 3-0 home defeat by Middlesbrough. Five days later he was part of a 2-0 victory over Birmingham but in the next game he conceded five at Bury. His run of 12 consecutive League and FA Cup appearances came to an end in March, with a 3-2 defeat at Bolton, and it was left to McClelland to see Fulham sink safely into Division Three.

COTTAGE COMMENT

1 FEBRUARY 1969:
Brian Williamson has waited six years for first-team football. He said: 'Now I've got it nothing is going to take it away from me.'

Fulham could not ask for a more positive attitude from their new goalkeeper. Knowing this, it was not surprising that Brian stayed on the field after gashing his arm in the first half of the match at Bury. It needed stitches, but they had to wait until after the game.

There are other unsung sacrifices in a footballer's life. Like having to leave his wife and daughters in Nottingham at mid-afternoon on Christmas Day while he motored down to London. To him it is all part of the game. He was determined to be in an undistracted mood for the match with Birmingham.

We all saw the result. His fine display including that 'miracle' save from Fred Pickering and a nice-looking '0' in the goals against column. The Williamson determination comes from hard experience.

Brian's last two games for Fulham came in the early part of the following season; against Southport and Barrow, both destined for relegation at the end of the campaign, and both destined eventually to lose League status. Fulham beat Southport 3-2, but lost 3-1 at Barrow. It seems Brian Williamson decided that enough was enough. He was not selected for first-team duty again, so he retired and became a security officer.

1970-97

PERRY DIGWEED, or Percy Dogwood as he was once famously called in an away programme, made just 15 League appearances for Fulham between 1977 and 1980. He was regarded as a fine prospect when he arrived at the Cottage, having been discovered playing football in a local park. Unfortunately for Perry, however, his arrival more or less coincided with that of Gerry Peyton and, having made his League debut in a 2-0 home defeat by Bolton Wanderers on 3 January 1977, he did not appear in the first team again until May 1979.

Perry did replace Gerry on a temporary basis during the 1979-80 season when, having played in the first game of that disastrous Division Two

Above: Perry Digweed.

Opposite: Laurence Batty.

Although I spent most of my time with Brighton, I started as a youngster with Fulham and made my debut playing alongside Bobby Moore and George Best. Besty spoke at my testimonial dinner at Brighton and I still have the odd jar with him from time to time.

As I was not getting regular first-team football at Fulham, I eventually asked for a transfer. I moved to Brighton and had a good career there. We had a couple of seasons in the First Division and reached the FA Cup Final in 1983. I didn't get to play in the Final or the Replay but I was in goal at Anfield for the Fifth Round match, which we won 2-1. There was a crowd of about 55,000 and most of them were expecting Liverpool to stuff us, even though we had beaten Manchester City 4-0 in the previous round. I really enjoyed the Anfield experience.

I am still a Fulham person at heart, though, and I live near the ground. I have been coming to a few games recently and I expect to come to a lot more in the future.

Perry Digweed

LAURENCE BATTY was born in February 1964 and joined Fulham 19 years later. Many of his teeage years were spent in Portugal where he learned the language and, between 1981 and 1983, played for Second Division Farense. Not long after joining Fulham, he was lent to Maidenhead United for a season, returning to make his League debut in a Division Two match against Grimsby at the Cottage in August 1985 which Fulham won 2-1. He replaced the injured Gerry Peyton, but lasted for just two games before Mark Grew took over until Gerry's return.

Laurence, known to one and all as 'George' because Terry Mancini thought Laurence was no name for a footballer (luckily, Perry Digweed had gone by this time) was not to see League action again until the end of the 1986-87 campaign when he took over from John Vaughan, but was unable to prevent the Cottagers from finishing the season in a lowly 18th place in Division Three. First-team opportunities continued to be restricted after that and Laurence played in only a dozen truly competitive games before his last in 1990, although he did make the odd appearance in competitions such as the Freight Rover Trophy.

campaign (an unusual 4-3 home win over Birmingham), he was recalled after Gerry was injured in a match against Notts County. Fulham were struggling badly, but Perry did rather well – keeping three clean sheets in that run of seven games. Gerry then returned to the fray and Perry played in only three more matches during that most awful of seasons – conceding five goals at Shrewsbury in the very last one as the Cottagers, along with Burnley and Charlton, were consigned to the Third.

Perry Digweed was born in Westminster during October 1959 and was therefore only 17 when he played his first League match. A winner of England Youth and Under-21 international honours, he might have expected to go on to much better things. In a sense he did – as Brighton & Hove Albion, then in the top division, paid a quite remarkable fee of £150,000 to secure his services in January 1981, and he went on to play around 200 games for the Seagulls. He now makes his living as a long-distance lorry driver.

**From the *Daily Telegraph*,
7 April 1997:**

The loudest laugh at many grounds on Saturday afternoons comes with the announcement of the Man of the Match award, but for once the sponsors at Woking got it absolutely right when they named Laurence Batty.

But for the goalkeeper's two magnificent saves in the closing minutes of a wind-ruined FA Trophy Semi-Final first leg, Woking would not be heading for Stevenage next week leading by Robin Taylor's goal after 31 seconds.

In his third match back after breaking a finger, Batty produced a breathtaking reflex save to tip Corey Browne's volley over. Then he went full length to save from Stevenage substitute Barry Hayles, who was subsequently denied again when he burst through.

Equally dominant in the air, Batty resisted Stevenage's best efforts when the Vauxhall Conference Champions pressed in the second half. 'It's a shame I don't drink the stuff,' said Batty, clutching his prize, a bottle of champagne. 'No, you can't have it. The missus likes it.'

Manager Ray Harford perhaps stands accused of failing to give young Laurence a fair crack of the whip, although for much of the time Jim Stannard inevitably stood between the young pretender and his chance of glory. Jim was not to be shifted easily, and eventually Laurence was obliged to seek his fortune elsewhere.

As most supporters will know, Batty became something of a hero with non-League Woking during the 1996-97 season. Together with fellow old boy Clive Walker he did very well against Coventry in two FA Cup games, and was even pictured on television sitting in a stand to watch Chelsea. At the end of March, with Woking going well in the Conference, he got his name on the scoresheet when he stepped up to take a spot-kick against Kidderminster in the absence of regular penalty-taker Walker. The following week he was again the star of the show when he helped to keep the hopes of his side alive in the FA Trophy Semi-Final first leg, and in May kept a clean sheet as his team lifted the trophy following extra time in the Wembley Final. Laurence Batty is alive and doing well.

Signed as a replacement for Gerry Peyton in the summer of 1986, **JOHN VAUGHAN** played first-team football for Fulham for just one season. It was, however, quite an eventful one.

John (22) had been with West Ham but, although he had won an FA Youth Cup-winner's medal and two Southern Junior Floodlit Cup medals while with the Hammers, had not managed to gain a place in the League side. He had travelled the country in search of a permanent home, visiting Charlton, Bristol Rovers and Wrexham for loan periods before arriving at Craven Cottage.

John was of less than average height for a goalkeeper but very agile, and turned in some very good performances. He began his spell at Fulham with a clean sheet (the first of 13 in a total of 52 League and Cup appearances) in a 0-0 draw at Rotherham, and all went well until his ninth game.

The 1986-87 season was to be a bad one for Fulham, with the worst still to come when the team travelled to Anfield for the first leg of a Littlewoods Cup Second Round match. Having comfortably disposed of Aldershot in the First Round, Fulham were confident if not of beating Liverpool then at least of putting up a creditable display. Manager Ray Lewington even arranged for the juniors to accompany the team to see how things should be done.

The juniors will presumably never forget the experience, and neither will Johnny Vaughan. Four first-half goals signalled Liverpool's intent, and these were followed by another half-dozen in the second period. No-one blamed John. Liverpool were unstoppable and many Fulham supporters actually enjoyed the game in spite of everything. In the end, the Kop was cheering Fulham and everyone thought of it simply as a night to remember, but it can't have done young Mr Vaughan's confidence a lot of good.

He recovered, however, and went on to have a fair season. True, he conceded five at home to Chester in January, and six at home to Port Vale in March, but these were extraordinary times for Fulham Football Club

with extinction threatening and the morale of players generally at an all-time low. It was to be some while before it would truly improve, but before the start of the 1987-88 season, Jim Stannard returned to the fold and John was consigned to the reserves.

Vaughan spent a frustrating second season at the Cottage. Batty had replaced him for the last two games of 1986-87 and John did not play for the first team again. From the Cottage he moved to Fourth Division Cambridge, where he became known as 'The Legend'. This started as a straightforward nickname, but when his side experienced an unprecedented run of success which almost culminated in promotion to the Premiership, the appellation stuck for good. John had proved himself to be an excellent keeper, and Cambridge fans remember him with the kind of affection Fulham fans still feel for Big Jim.

From Cambridge, John moved to Charlton. He then followed his old manager John Beck to Preston and on to Lincoln City. He was on loan to Colchester when Fulham visited Sincil Bank during 1996-97, but later returned to help Lincoln almost reach the play-offs.

*Opposite and top:
John Vaughan.*

LEE HARRISON was born in Billericay on 12 September 1971 and was with Leyton Orient as a schoolboy before signing for Charlton. He came on loan to Fulham in November 1991 and kept a clean sheet against Gillingham in the Autoglass Trophy, an event witnessed by a massive crowd of 1,108. Lee returned whence he came, but had loan spells with Gillingham, Welling United and Fulham once more before signing at the Cottage in August 1993.

Jim Stannard was of course almost ever-present for several seasons and Lee actually made his League debut as a substitute after Jim was dismissed for causing an opposing forward to take a dive in a 1-1 draw with Lincoln City in November 1994. Lee then played in a 1-1 draw at Gillingham in Round Two of the FA Cup in December. He kept very well in this Kentish encounter, making one superb save and earning the praise of Chairman Hill for his performance.

FIRST PERSON

I enjoyed my time at Fulham, especially the loan periods. I played mainly in Autoglass games, but at least these gave me a chance to be seen by a few people!

By the time I signed for Fulham, Jim Stannard had of course been at the Cottage for many years. I didn't get too many chances (Jim was not the easiest keeper to push out!) but when he moved to Gillingham I naturally hoped for better things for myself. It was not to be, however, as Ian Branfoot decided to sign Tony Lange and I was still mostly on the sidelines.

The Fulham side was struggling, of course, but we all knew the club had potential. I was sorry to leave but I'm very happy at Barnet. I particularly enjoyed our home game against Fulham last season, and I even enjoyed hearing the Fulham fans having a bit of a go at me! You always want to do well against your old club but I also wanted my old team-mates to have a good game, so I was happy enough with the 2-2 scoreline.

I hear it's all been happening down at the Cottage at the moment, and I wish everyone there well for the future.

Lee Harrison

Lee made several more appearances towards the end of the 1994-95 season, and although he kept quite well he did have a couple of unfortunate experiences. He was sent off during the 1-0 victory over Hartlepool in April and a week later conceded five in a rather sad defeat at Layer Road.

With Tony Lange brought in as first-choice keeper at the start of the 1995-96 campaign, Lee Harrison's Fulham days were numbered. He made just five more League appearances, but even so, his record is rather a good one. In all, he conceded an average of a goal a game in League and FA Cup encounters, but in July 1996 he left for Barnet, where he has since done very well.

PASSING THROUGH

This section covers 24 goalkeepers all of whom, for one reason or another, failed to reach double figures for Fulham in terms of League and/or Cup appearances.

At the beginning comes **HS CURLING**. Old HS made his first Southern League Division Two appearance in January 1899 as a temporary replacement for Albert Maile. Fulham lost that encounter 2-0 at Southall and a week later, with HS again between the posts, they drew 1-1 at home to Uxbridge.

Early in the following season Curling played in three more games, the last of which – a 3-3 draw at Brentford – proved to be his swansong as far as first-team football for Fulham was concerned. It was a shame really, because his five Southern League matches had resulted in two defeats, two draws and just one win – and he failed to keep a clean sheet in any of them.

And now for a somewhat strange tale, the reasons for which are, sadly, lost in the mists of time. Between 1899 and 1904 Fulham had on their books a very fine inside-right called **DAVID LLOYD**. During his time at the Cottage he played in 38 Southern League games and 11 FA Cup games, scoring 24 goals. He left Fulham for a while to go off to the Boer War, and came back as a centre-half. Shortly before that, however, he played in goal against Maidenhead in a Southern League game at the Cottage in April 1901. Nobody seems to know why – perhaps the horse-buses were on strike and regular keeper Jack Head

could not get to the ground – but David donned the jersey and kept a clean sheet while his colleagues put nine past the Maidonians at the other end!

Keeping goal against Maidenhead seems not to have been exciting enough for David Lloyd, so off he went to fight the Boers, presumably hoping that Head would in future turn up to do his duty for Fulham on a regular basis. His hopes were largely justified, as Jack missed only two games over the next two Southern League (Division Two) campaigns. When Jack did go

Below: Tynesider Fred Biggar, who made his Fulham debut in 1903.

AWOL in October 1901, his place was taken by **C RANCE**, who featured in a 2-1 win at Wycombe Wanderers and a 2-0 defeat at Brighton before disappearing from the scene without a home appearance to his credit.

Jack Fryer took over from Head as prime custodian at the start of the 1903-04 season, and for a while **FRED BIGGAR** served as his deputy. Born in Blaydon-on-Tyne in 1877, Fred remained at Fulham for just one season before moving on to Watford, and later Rochdale, but he did manage to make a total of nine first-team appearances during his brief sojourn at the Cottage. Prior to his signing for Fulham, he had been with Sheffield United as deputy to Fatty Foulke, so had a little experience of the big time. On his debut, Fulham beat New Brompton 1-0, and this proved to be the first of five clean sheets in Southern League Division One and FA Cup games. Fred then handed over the deputy's role to **HENRY CLUTTERBUCK**.

Henry joined Fulham towards the end of his career. He had previously played for Hereford Thistle, Small Heath, Queens Park Rangers, Grimsby Town, Chesterfield and New Brompton and (with apologies to any Clutterbucks who happen to be reading this) his unusual appellation had probably caused a certain amount of merriment at all those locations. Henry was, however, pretty adept in his chosen vocation. Described as a 'sound, cool and clever custodian', he had been first choice at Small Heath, QPR and Chesterfield. He played just three first-team games for Fulham in the 1904-05 season before deciding upon retirement. These resulted in a goalless draw at home to Southampton, a 2-1 defeat at Watford and a 3-0 defeat at home to West Ham. Then it was goodbye to Henry James Clutterbuck.

Henry's successor as Jack Fryer's Southern League deputy was another much travelled goalkeeper. **FRED THOMPSON** was born in 1876 and played for Sunderland, Bury, Bolton, Luton and Portsmouth before joining Fulham. He had been in goal for Bury when, in 1900, they beat Southampton 4-0 in the FA Cup Final played at Crystal Palace, and a year earlier had represented the North versus the South in a trial match. This resulted in a 4-4 draw, a high-scoring game that probably signalled the end of any international ambitions for Fred.

Thompson was to play only five first-team games for Fulham, all in the 1905-06 season. The four Southern League Division One games resulted in victories for the Cottagers, who were to finish top of the table. Fred's first match was a 2-1 win at Brighton in November 1905, while his last was in February 1906 – an FA Cup Second Round encounter at Nottingham Forest which Fulham lost 3-1. Fred left at the end of the season to join his seventh club, Norwich City. He just failed to make it into double figures by the end of his career as, after Norwich, he managed to sign for only two more teams – Clapton Orient and Hartlepools.

The 1906-07 season saw Fryer with yet another deputy, this time in the shape of **WILL HORNE**. Will hailed from Plymouth and had been an Argyle goalkeeper since 1903. But Fulham were being tipped as possible new members of the Football League, so Will decided to throw in his lot with the men from the metropolis and move from the tranquillity of the West Country to the thrills and spills of London life.

It availed him not. Fryer held his place throughout Fulham's last Southern League season and, although Jack was badly injured in a match towards the end of the campaign, Will obviously decided it was not worth waiting around for League action. Having made just two appearances, in a 2-1 home win over Reading and a 4-1 defeat at West Ham on the last day of the season, he packed his bags and returned to Home Park – where he remained until 1915, re-establishing himself as one of Argyle's most noted players.

Leslie Skene became Fulham's first-choice goalkeeper when the Football League was entered in 1907 and, for a fee of £15, **HERBERT CROSSTHWAITE** was signed as cover. Born in Preston in April 1887, Herbert had played for Blackpool and was later to establish himself with Exeter, Birmingham and Stoke City. For now, though, he was a Fulham player, and was to be another who made just two League appearances. The first resulted in a 2-1 home victory over Burnley and the second, the last game of the 1907-08 season, a win with a similar scoreline over Glossop North End. With Fryer once more on the scene, Fulham decided to let his deputy go west a year later, and he moved to Exeter. Herbert Crossthwaite later joined Birmingham City Police and rose to the rank of inspector.

During the 1909-10 season, both Skene and Fryer suffered injuries, and just after Christmas the Cottagers found themselves without a custodian. **RUDOLPH O'DONNELL**, who was born in India and had played football for the Army, answered the call. Rudolph was an experienced and very capable amateur whose 'day job' was music: he worked for the Army as a bandmaster. Borrowed from Reading, he featured in three matches – a 3-2 defeat at Hull, a 3-1 defeat at Derby County, and finally a 2-0 home win over Stockport County – before returning. Rudolph died in 1961.

The advent of Arthur Reynolds towards the end of the 1909-10 season, combined with the signing of Wilf Nixon, meant that Fulham had no need of occasional keepers until November 1913. Then Arthur was injured and **HUGH McDONALD** was signed. Hugh was born in Kilwinning (a fine birthplace for a highly motivated footballer) in Ayrshire in 1884 and came to the Cottage via Woolwich Arsenal,

Brighton, Woolwich Arsenal (again), Oldham Athletic and Bradford.

He had been the main goalkeeper at most of these clubs, but at Fulham made only eight appearances in the space of less than two months. The first was a most acceptable 6-1 drubbing of his old club Arsenal, the last a 2-1 defeat at Leeds City on Christmas Day. Arthur Reynolds then bounced back, and McDonald left for Bristol Rovers. He later became a publican in Plumstead and died at an early age in 1920.

After the Great War, Reynolds was Fulham's principal goalkeeping hero. He was virtually ever-present for five seasons and hardly anyone could get a look-in until 1925. **FRED WHALLEY** was, however, something of a hero in his own right. Born in Salford in October 1898 he had enlisted in the North Lancashire Regiment at the age of 15 and seen active service in France. He played football for the Army, and after the war signed for Preston North End.

Opposite: The Cottage was the meat in an Argyle sandwich for Will Horne.

Above: War hero Fred Whalley was a northerner who arrived from Leeds.

A reserve at Deepdale, he moved to Grimsby for first-team action, and later to Leeds United, before coming to the Cottage towards the end of his career in March 1924. He played one game towards the end of the 1923-24 season – a 2-1 defeat at Leicester City – and eight more in the following campaign, keeping a clean sheet in four of them. On retirement from the game, Fred joined the police. He died in 1976.

LEN BOOT joined Fulham in 1925, and played in the first three games of the 1925-26 season. He conceded eight goals and gave way to Tom McKenna. Born in West Bromwich in November 1899, he had played for Huddersfield before joining Fulham. Ernie Beecham was about to begin his custodial reign but, after his less than wonderful start, Len had another half-dozen games in which to attempt to make an impression.

Unfortunately he didn't. He kept one clean sheet, but Fulham were victorious in only one of the nine games in which he played a part and Len was soon on his way back north. He joined Bradford City and later Nottingham Forest but never became a regular choice.

Beecham was to give other hopeful Cottage keepers fewer chances to shine even than Reynolds. When Ernie received his dreadful injury in November 1928, his duties for the rest of the season fell upon Bill Mason – except for one game in March 1929, when

ARTHUR WILLIAM MEESON stood proud between the posts. Arthur (born in Headington in 1904) had played for Oxford City and Arsenal before joining Fulham. He had recently won an amateur international cap but had been unable to break into Arsenal's League side.

It may be a little unkind to suggest it, but there were probably quite a few people at Craven Cottage on 9 March 1929 who wished he had failed to break into Fulham's League side too. The Cottagers were cruising to a Division Three (South) victory over Southend at half-time, confident they would be able to extend their two-goal advantage and quite oblivious to the possibility of Arthur letting in four goals during the second period. But he did. It proved to be his one and only game, and he later moved to Lincoln City.

The only other goalkeeper to make less than ten first-team appearances before the world was again thrown into conflict was **LEN BROOKS**. Born in 1913 in England's smallest town, Manningtree in Essex, Len was a butler who played for Fleet in the Aldershot League on his day off. He signed for Fulham as an amateur sometime in 1935 and badly injured his wrist after a quarter of an hour in his first reserve-team game, completing the rest of the match one-handed. His one-handed work was apparently remarkably good and he stayed on as cover for Alf Tootill.

He played just twice in Fulham's first team, however, his first appearance coming towards the end of the 1935-36 season – a 1-0 home defeat by Swansea Town – and his final one being a 5-2 home victory over Nottingham Forest in January 1937. Len moved to Bournemouth later that year, and played regularly for the Cherries until the outbreak of hostilities.

In common with many other clubs, Fulham had a number of guest players during the Second World War. For this reason, any goalkeeper who happened to stroll down Stevenage Road in search of a game during the war years is not covered by this volume. Neither are keepers such as Harry Duke, a slightly unpredictable Norwich City player who nonetheless gave the odd brilliant performance during his 101 guest appearances for Fulham. However, Llanelli-born **OSWALD EVANS**, who joined Fulham during February 1946 and played 13 times prior to the beginning of the official resumption of League football, gets more than a mention because he featured in one postwar encounter.

Ossie had done rather well in the Fulham goal during that last Football League South season. According to Jim Sims, he was well on the way to becoming a cult hero as he helped the Cottagers into a respectable eighth place by the time the campaign was at an end.

Ossie was a large goalkeeper. He was, in fact, very large indeed, weighing in at around 20 stone and making our Jim look positively sylph-like. He made his Second Division debut

in a game at Bury. And what a debut (and, as it turned out, final League appearance) it was to prove.

Fulham supporters were doubtless optimistic about their team's chances in the League after the barren wartime years, and were probably quite unable to believe their ears as the very first football results crackled over the wireless. Ronnie Rooke had scored twice, but the real action had been at the other end. Poor old Ossie had seen the ball pass his fat frame seven times, Fulham were humiliated, and Ossie's League career was at an end. Hinton took over for the next game (away to West Ham) and let in only three.

LARRY GAGE made half a dozen appearances for Fulham towards the end of the war years. Afterwards he moved to Aldershot, went to

Opposite: Former Gunner Arthur Meeson cost £175 in December 1928, but his one Fulham game also proved expensive in goal terms.

Above: A positively svelte-looking Oswald Evans also played just one League game.

MATCH ACTION

Following a 2-2 home draw with Brentford in March 1946 (towards the end of the last wartime season) this appeared in a Sunday newspaper:

Fulham's new goalkeeper, Evans, again played a useful game. He has learned the art of positioning himself and some of his saves looked easy only because of his sound judgment a second or so in advance of the shots.

kept a clean sheet in Fulham's 2-0 home win over West Ham. The Cottagers were promoted as Champions (it *can* happen) and Larry Gage was one of the 11 heroes of the hour.

That proved to be Larry's last first-team game for Fulham. After a further season of reserve-team obscurity, he transferred to Gillingham in June 1950 and made 40 League appearances for the Kent club.

Born in Durham in August 1935, **BRIAN RONSON** played his first and last League games for Fulham in March 1954. The Cottagers were experiencing their second season back in Division Two and, after an appalling start, were by now going quite well. First-choice keeper Ian Black then broke his arm and Brian was brought in for a home game against Blackburn Rovers. Fulham lost 3-2 but Brian survived for a trip to Doncaster, which resulted in a 2-2 draw. He did not survive this time, and Frank Elliott replaced him thereafter.

Left: Two-game Brian Ronson.

Opposite: A beaming Martin Townsend.

Canada, and then returned to Fulham in August 1948. A Londoner born in September 1922, he found himself the fourth-choice goalkeeper at the Cottage when the new season commenced and there seemed to be few opportunities for glory. But, as has been noted elsewhere in the literature of the sport, football is a funny game.

Hinton had started in goal in this most momentous of Fulham League seasons, but after ten games his place had been taken by Doug Flack. As 1948-49 progressed it became clear that the Cottagers had a real chance of promotion to the top flight for the first time, and Doug was doing well. Sadly for him, however, he sustained an injury with just three games to go, and in came Larry.

Fulham had won their previous four matches and, with Flack having conceded just two goals in these encounters, Gage had a lot to live up to. He started well. With 40,000 souls present at the Cottage, he helped his side beat Brentford 2-1 in the first game, and a week later took part in a 1-1 draw at Tottenham before a crowd of 51,199. Larry obviously enjoyed playing against London teams as, in the last game of the season, he

FIRST PERSON

Even though I only played in three first-team games, I'll never forget my years with Fulham. I have no regrets at all, even though the results could have been better!

I could hardly believe it when I was drafted into the first team for the game at Turf Moor. Tony and Dave were both injured, so it was me or Roger Durdle, both juniors. I got the job and I think I played quite well at Burnley – at least, the Gentlemen of the Press thought so – but I know I made a couple of errors in the next game against Arsenal.

I was very nervous in front of our home crowd and, with the game level at one apiece, I called Bill Dodgin for a short goal-kick. Unfortunately, I didn't hit the ball hard enough and while Bill was waiting for it to arrive, Joe Baker popped up and dispossessed him, and that led to goal number two for Arsenal. But still, I was only 17 at the time.

I get to see Fulham occasionally and I was delighted when they won promotion last season. I wish them the very best of luck.

Martin Townsend

Ronson had failed to set the Cottage alight, and there were to be no more first-team games for him. He remained a Fulham player until the summer of 1956, however, playing in the occasional reserve-team game – including one at Plymouth Argyle in March of that year. He then moved to Southend, Norwich City, and on to Peterborough where he made 50 League appearances.

Almost ten years after Ronson's two appearances, **MARTIN TOWNSEND** went one better. He played in three games in September 1963, conceding a total of 13 goals. Born in Romford in June 1946, Martin was only 17 when he temporarily took over from Dave Underwood, who in turn had been playing in place of Martin's mentor Tony Macedo, the latter being incarcerated within St Stevens hospital for a knee operation.

Martin was between the posts for a 4-1 First Division defeat at Burnley, during which he actually played very well, and then nervously returned to the Cottage to feature in a match which resulted in an identical defeat by

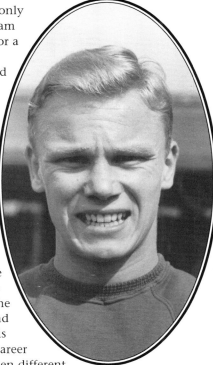

Arsenal. His only other first-team outing was for a League Cup game at Third Division Colchester 11 days later, which resulted in a 5-3 victory for the Essex side.

Martin had, of course, come into the side long before he was ready and the rest of his footballing career may have been different

FIRST PERSON

After the Arsenal game, Tony Macedo wrote to Martin Townsend from his hospital bed:

Tony Macedo
St Steven's Hospital
SW10
15 September 1963

Dear Martin,
Let me say first how glad I was to hear of your selection for the first team. All my thoughts were with you that night at Burnley. I knew you would not let them down, and Beddy assured me after that game that you had done very well indeed.

Today I have read the reports on Saturday's game against Arsenal, I expect everybody has tried to be as sympathetic as possible to you, and you must be sick of people giving you advice lately.

I don't believe for one minute that the result of the game was due solely to your lack of experience, Martin. You have been unfortunate in coming into a side that is

suffering from lack of confidence, and a long string of injuries, therefore every man in the team is below his usual standard, and this in itself naturally puts a great pressure on you.

All these things you will learn to realise yourself one day, but at the moment Martin you must learn from what is happening to you. I think I have known you long enough to know that you will keep a level head. You must under no circumstances pay any attention to the Press. I have told you that before, and remember that everyone at the club will help you to make the grade, which I have no doubt you will one day achieve.

Remember what I told you about self confidence. You have the ability, Martin, otherwise you would not be where you are. Don't forget what has happened, but learn from it. Remember, I had a worse experience than you against Manchester United in that Semi-Final.
Good luck Martin.
Hope to see you soon,
Tony

had he not been given such a baptism of fire. In the event, he later moved to Guildford City, and then played for Stevenage and Hastings. He now works for a local newspaper in Romford.

Gerry Peyton was about to begin his long career as Fulham's number one goalkeeper when **RICHARD TEALE** also signed for the Cottagers. Born in Millam in February 1952, Richard played for Walton and Hersham, where he won an FA Amateur Cup-winner's medal, Slough Town and Queens Park Rangers (one First Division appearance) before Alec Stock secured his signature for Fulham. He played in the first two games of the 1976-77 season, a 2-2 draw at home to Nottingham Forest and a 3-1 defeat at Burnley, before Peter Mellor returned for his last few Fulham games. Then Richard had one more match, a 3-2 defeat at Blackpool, before Gerry made his debut.

Gerry played in the next four – and then came Richard's last two, with three goals conceded at home to Millwall and another three at Cardiff. Teale stayed on until the end of the season but, having conceded 14 goals in his five appearances and with Peyton now firmly established in Fulham's Division Two side, he moved to League new boys Wimbledon. After 15 appearances for the Dons he returned to Slough, later playing for Staines and Carshalton Athletic.

With Peyton dominating and Jim Stannard largely deputising for him when he was not on loan to Southend or Charlton, Fulham themselves resorted to borrowing a couple of keepers when needed. The need arose in 1984-85, when they borrowed **IAIN HESFORD** from Sheffield Wednesday, and again early in the following season when **MARK GREW** arrived from Ipswich.

Iain played just three games in January and February 1985 – keeping a clean sheet in the middle one, at home to Brighton – before Gerry returned to the side, while Mark played his part in three defeats and a draw in September of the same year. As far as Mark was concerned, the saving grace was that he kept a clean sheet in the goalless draw at Crystal Palace and only let in five altogether.

Both of these itinerant goalkeepers then returned to their home clubs before going on loan elsewhere and, eventually, on to more settled careers. Grew became Port Vale's first-choice goalkeeper, later becoming youth-team manager, while Hesford went on to Sunderland and then Hull City, before moving to Maidstone (where he featured in that club's last League game) and on to Hong Kong.

During February 1991, Fulham signed another player as cover for Jim Stannard. **TONY PARKS**, born in Hackney in January 1963, had started as an apprentice with Tottenham and made 37 League appearances at White Hart Lane. After a couple of loan periods, with Oxford United and Gillingham respectively, he moved to Brentford in August 1988 and had a further 71 League outings for the Bees. Tony played in just two Division Three games for Fulham – a 1-1 home draw with Reading and a 3-0 defeat at Bolton Wanderers. Then Jim came back and Tony left for Upton Park.

Jim missed very few games during this period but in 1992 **ALAN GOUGH** (born in Watford, March 1971) was signed – initially on loan – from Portsmouth. He made his debut in a 2-1 defeat at Bournemouth in September and then, three days later, featured in a 1-1 draw at home to Swansea. Alan had to wait until March 1993 for another chance, when he was between the posts at Burnden Park and conceded the only goal of the match. That proved to be Alan's final first-team game, and he left for Gillingham in August 1993. He made no League appearances

at the Priestfield Stadium, and was last heard of playing for Dublin side Shelbourne.

On 8 April 1995, Fulham were at home to Hartlepool. The Cottagers were coming to the end of their first ever season in what everyone still thought of as the Fourth Division and, although it had not been quite as bad as some had feared, it had hardly qualified as the most exhilarating of campaigns. The match with Hartlepool was going to be a routine affair and, as he sat patiently on the bench just in case of mishap, **JOHN GREGORY** no doubt confidently expected Lee Harrison to play for a full 90 minutes.

John, born in Hounslow in 1977, had come up through the ranks but had not yet signed professional forms. He may have been hoping one day to emulate Big Jim, who was shortly to end his Fulham career with a massive 430 appearances to his credit, but he did not expect Lee to be sent off during the Hartlepool game. Lee was given his marching orders, however, and Gregory made what was to be his only first-team appearance – as a substitute goalkeeper in a 1-0 Fulham victory. Then he went to Woking, and later to Kingstonian. It really is a funny old game.

CLASS OF 1997-98

ANDRE ARENDSE

The decision to release Tony Lange during the summer of 1997 meant that Fulham had just one keeper capable of donning the first-team jersey. Accordingly, a replacement for Tony was needed and Micky Adams, at last with money to spend, selected South African international Andre Arendse to fill the vacancy.

Thirty-year-old Andre began his football career with Cape amateur club Vasco de Gama. Had he been born a few years later his career might have turned out very differently, but as it was he eventually became a star keeper with Cape Town Spurs, helping them to a League and Cup Double in 1995.

Andre's abilities were soon to become more widely recognised and, as South Africa began to emerge from the football wilderness, he became his country's regular goalkeeper. He signed on at the Cottage when his contract with Cape Town Spurs expired and, having made almost 30 international appearances, went straight into Fulham's reserve side.

His first-team debut was delayed in part by inevitable work-permit complications and Andre found himself in the strange position of

Andre is a very agile goalkeeper and an impressive shot-stopper. He is also a very dedicated trainer, always working extremely hard and setting an excellent example to all the other players.

He has of course been called away frequently for training sessions and for matches with the South African national side. Naturally this has involved a lot of long-distance travelling and has caused disruption for Andre as far as his goalkeeping for Fulham is concerned. There is also the question of his work permit: things would have been somewhat easier on this front had he been an Italian playing in *Serie A*. His journeys would have been shorter, too – I should know!

At the time of writing, Andre's long-term future is a little uncertain. He is a Fulham player and an asset to the squad, and I would like to keep him with us, but in the end it will come down to what is best for the player himself.

Ray Wilkins

playing in a World Cup qualifying match in Johannesburg in front of an estimated audience of 80,000 before returning to England and the delights of Optimum Interiors Capital League matches – which are normally witnessed by a couple of dozen retired persons and a bored dog.

Such are the vagaries of life for the professional footballer, especially when he has signed for a club which is attempting to establish itself in Division Two, while suddenly having seemingly limitless resources at its disposal.

Andre finally made his first-team debut on Tuesday 16 September and conceded the only goal of the game as Fulham lost at home to Wolves in the Coca-Cola Cup. Four days later he played at Southend, where his side again lost 1-0, this being followed by the second leg of the cup tie at Molineux and yet another 1-0 defeat for the Cottagers.

Andre's fourth game, at Wigan, ended 2-1 to the home side, which was a pity because half of the world's press had descended on Lancashire following the departure of Micky

Adams and the appointment of Kevin Keegan and Ray Wilkins. A week later Fulham's newest keeper at last took part in a victory, but he still failed to keep a clean sheet as Oldham were beaten 3-1.

He played in just three more games before the end of 1997, these being a 1-1 draw at Millwall, a slightly surprising win by the odd goal in five at Bristol Rovers, and an unsurprising win by the odd goal in three at Margate in the First Round of the FA Cup – a game for which Andre had given up the chance to play for his country in a friendly against Germany.

Andre Arendse did not manage to keep a clean sheet in any of his eight games. Mark Walton had returned to the side to cover for the South African's international duties and had kept his place for a game or two, but the new management team clearly felt that the goalkeeping position was still in need of strengthening and they were hot on the trail of Southampton's Maik Taylor – for whom they were about to pay the best part of three quarters of a million pounds.

MAIK TAYLOR

Maik Stephan Taylor was born in Hildesheim, Germany in September 1971. The son of an English father and German mother, he played as a 12-year-old sweeper in north German schoolboy football. He later followed in his father's military footsteps, converted to a goalkeeper and eventually played for the Army and for the Combined Services.

Still a member of the Armed Forces, Maik then joined Farnborough, with whom he won a Beazer Homes Premier Division Championship medal, having earlier made ten loan appearances for Basingstoke. By this time he had come to the attention of Barnet manager Ray Clemence who, recognising a

FIRST PERSON

Maik has done very well since he joined us from Southampton. As is the case with all players who are new to a squad, it takes a little time to adjust to the fresh set-up, especially when you have not been playing regular first-team football.

Maik was of course playing regularly in the Premiership towards the end of last season, and the experience he gained at the Dell has stood him in good stead. At around six foot three he has tremendous presence in the goalmouth and he is a great athlete. I know the supporters have been generally impressed with his performance, and the good news is that I believe there is still scope for improvement – especially as we have the Cat himself, Peter Bonetti, as a specialist goalkeeping coach. With his previous experience of working with Ray Clemence, plus help and advice from Peter, Maik could turn out to be one of Fulham's best ever keepers.

Ray Wilkins

good goalkeeper when he saw one, promptly bought Lance Corporal Taylor out of the Army for £700 and signed him for the Hertfordshire side in June 1995.

Maik did very well at Underhill and was soon on his way back to Hampshire, this time to join Premiership team Southampton who signed him for a £500,000 fee at the end of December 1996. Selected to play in a League game at Middlesbrough on 11 January 1997, Maik kept a clean sheet while Jim Magilton scored from the spot to give Southampton three valuable points.

He continued to impress and was ever-present for the rest of the 1996-97 League season, notching up further clean sheets against Wimbledon, Newcastle, Leeds, West Ham, Sunderland and Blackburn. He had, however, lost his regular place in the side by the time Keegan and Wilkins made the bid which brought him to the Cottage.

Quite a lot has happened since Ray Clemence took me for a one and a half hour training session, and then signed me for Barnet. He had not actually seen me play before, but I must have done well because he soon offered me a contract. In point of fact, I owe Ray a great deal. I had not received any specialist coaching in goalkeeping before I joined Barnet, so Ray really taught me the basics. He also went through everything after each match, which was very valuable indeed.

I enjoyed my time at Underhill and I have some good memories, but I remember feeling a bit intimidated when we visited the Cottage. We came here a couple of times, the first visit resulting in a 1-1 draw when Gary Brazil scored the equaliser for Fulham, and the second a 2-0 defeat for Barnet – with Mike Conroy scoring a real cracker. Even then, I felt that Fulham had a great deal of potential. They were a powerful side and more physical than their reputation suggested, and the whole atmosphere of Craven Cottage made me think that things could only improve.

I never expected to end up here, of course, and I was delighted when I had the chance to move from Barnet to Southampton, the club I had supported as a lad in Germany. I will admit that I did not really want to leave the Dell and the chance to play more Premiership football, but Fulham were prepared to pay a substantial fee and Southampton needed the money. I would not have considered dropping two divisions had I not believed that Fulham would themselves eventually be heading for the Premiership, and I am now more than happy that I made the move.

It may take a bit of time, but with the players we have, and with a little patience from our supporters, I know we can do really well. Things are already looking up, and it's good to see so many more people turning up for home and away games. Last season I played in front of more than 55,000 people at Old Trafford. We can't get that many into Craven Cottage, but who knows what the future may bring?

Speaking of the future, one or two people have asked which national side – England or Germany – I would like to play for if I ever had the chance. My answer, quite naturally I think, is that I'd be absolutely delighted to be asked to play for either! But all I'm really thinking about right now is helping Fulham to climb the League ladder.

Maik Taylor

Taylor made his Fulham debut on 18 November at home to York City. The Minstermen were in third position in the Division Two table and a hard game was envisaged. And so it proved, with Fulham unable to scramble anything better than a 1-1 draw, but Maik soon had the crowd on his side – especially when, diving at full stretch, he almost saved the penalty which gave the visitors a half-time lead.

Three days later Maik was again between the posts as Fulham entertained a Gillingham side to which Jim Stannard had been restored. The Fulham crowd naturally gave Jim a rousing reception which he duly acknowledged, but it was to be the Fulham goalkeeper's night.

In truth, he did not have a great deal to do as, once the visitors had been reduced to ten men, the ball remained stubbornly in Gillingham's half of the field and it was Jim who had his work cut out. The result was three goals for Fulham – and Maik Taylor's first clean sheet for his new club.

The Cottagers took only one point from their next three League games, losing 3-1 at Preston and 2-0 at Carlisle with a 1-1 draw at home to Micky Adams' Brentford sandwiched in-between, but on 6 December they did manage to scramble a 1-0 victory over Southend in the Cup.

Maik was between the posts in all of these games and was part of the end-of-year surge as Fulham – with the new players now beginning to settle in and play well together – completed 1997 with a hat-trick of wins, culminating in a 1-0 victory over high-flying Bristol City (Maik's fifth clean sheet for Fulham, if you include the 1-0 win over Watford in the Auto Windscreens Shield) before more than 13,000 fans. One wonders what Albert Maile would have made of it all.

MARK WALTON

ark Walton was born in June 1969 and was on the books of Swansea City and Luton Town before making his League debut with Colchester United under manager Roger Brown. Mark had played for the Welsh Under-21 side and he did well at Layer Road – so well that Norwich City paid a £75,000 fee for him in August 1989. However, he played only 22 games for the Canaries, where he mainly covered for Bryan Gunn.

After Carrow Road, Mark wandered the country in search of regular first-team football, playing for both Bolton and his hometown club Merthyr before signing for Fulham. His first game was in August 1996, a 1-0 home win over Hereford United – the side that was to finish bottom of the table at the season's

FIRST PERSON

I'll certainly never forget the game at Mansfield last season, when we secured promotion. The atmosphere was tremendous and I was so pleased for the rest of the team, and of course for all the supporters.

Fulham is clearly going from strength to strength and it looks very much as though it really *will* be a big club one day. The bigger the club, the larger the squad and I am pleased to a be a part of the set-up, although I would naturally love to play first-team football on a regular basis.

Everyone at the club knows that changes are inevitable, and it's up to each and every one of us to prove that he is worth his place. In three or four years' time it will be interesting to look at a photo of the 1997-98 squad to see just how many of the players are still with Fulham…

Mark Walton

end. This proved to be the first of 15 clean sheets in a total of 31 League and Coca-Cola Cup outings in 1996-97.

Tony Lange was between the posts for part of this most memorable of recent seasons but Mark featured in the last 16 matches, during which he kept his goal intact on eight occasions. It had been some years since he had experienced the 'big match atmosphere' but Mark appeared quite unaffected by all the excitement as Fulham headed for promotion from Division Three and very nearly won the Championship.

Mark Walton would not be described as a spectacular goalkeeper and he was ably assisted in the great promotion battle of 1996-97 by some excellent defensive performances from the likes of Nick Cusack

'Wally' is a lovely Welsh bloke. He's brilliant in the dressing room and, although he has a very gentle voice for such a big man, you can always hear him laughing, making jokes and singing. His whole attitude is excellent for team spirit, and it helped us all during the promotion campaign.

Wally joined us in the summer of 1996. He weighed in at around 19 stone and, when he dropped to the ground in pre-season games, he used to leave an enormous crater! He worked very hard on his fitness, however, earned himself a contract and then went straight into the League side because Tony Lange had a groin injury. In that first game against Hereford, he did very well indeed – moving off his line at the right time and taking a good deal of pressure off the defence. He kept his place for two more games, before sustaining an injury. After that he alternated with Tony until the promotion run-in, and really distinguished himself.

Our defence was playing well, but Wally was also growing in confidence. He began to really command the area and this gave added confidence to everyone at the back. He saved us at Carlisle when Warren Aspinall was clean through and, when we were beaten 1-0 by Northampton he saved us from a much more embarrassing scoreline.

Simon Morgan

and Mark Blake. He did, however, show great competence during that campaign – and it must be remembered that some keepers are inclined to give their more spectacular performances only when their positional sense is at fault in the first place. Mark did very well in 1996-97 and he started 1997-98 in pretty much the same vein, conceding just five goals in the first seven League games before the arrival of Andre Arendse.

Had it not been for a very strange 4-4 draw with Wycombe Wanderers in the Coca-Cola Cup, Mark's average during his Fulham career to 31 December 1997 would have been a remarkable 0.84 goals conceded per game. That's not bad for a goalkeeper who, 18 months earlier, had been struggling to find a home with a League side!

Shortly after the interview opposite, Mark's desire for front-line action took him on loan to Gillingham in February 1998, with a view to a permanent £40,000 transfer. Ray Wilkins was disappointed to see him go. 'He's given tremendous effort since we've been here, but he's at the age when he needs to be playing first-team football. We can't guarantee that, so we wish him the best of luck. He's not only a very good goalkeeper but a super guy.'

As it transpired, Mark played just one game, doing his former team-mates a favour by beating table-toppers Watford, before a failure to agree terms led to a swift return. Ironically, the man to benefit was Jim Stannard, who returned to the fray and single-handedly secured another notable Gills victory – this time against Bristol City at Ashton Gate!

ANORAKS' CORNER

There are three kinds of lies – lies, damned lies and statistics. So wrote Benjamin Disraeli, the well known custodian of Beaconsfield. As far as goalkeepers are concerned, statistics can in any case give only a general indication of levels of performance and they are therefore to be treated with extreme caution. Let's face it, the best keeper in the world would have struggled behind some of the defensive line-ups produced by Fulham over the years.

Every effort has been made to ensure accuracy in the tables below, but statistical errors are a bit like goals at Craven Cottage – they sometimes creep in when you least expect them.

The stats refer to all goalkeepers who played for Fulham between 10 September 1898 and 28 December 1997, and cover all games played in the Southern League (Divisions One and Two, including test matches), the Football League (including play-offs), the Football Association Cup and the Football League Cup with its various sponsors.

ALPHABETICAL LIST OF FULHAM GOALKEEPERS

NAME	FIRST MATCH	LAST MATCH	TOTAL PLAYED	GOALS CONCEDED	AVERAGE
Arendse, Andre**	16 September 1997	16 November 1997	8	10	1.250
Batty, Laurence	26 August 1985	11 December 1990	13	20	1.538
Beecham, Ernie	5 December 1925	3 October 1931	185	357	1.929
Biggar, Fred	19 September 1903	18 April 1904	9	7	0.777
Black, Ian	19 August 1950	16 November 1957	277	471	1.700
Boot, Leonard	29 August 1925	28 November 1925	9	15	1.666
Brooks, Leonard	25 April 1936	2 January 1937	2	3	1.500
Clutterbuck, Henry	8 October 1904	17 April 1905	3	5	1.666
Crossthwaite, Herbert	8 February 1908	29 April 1908	2	2	1.000
Curling, HS	14 January 1899	4 November 1899	5	11	2.200
Digweed, Perry	3 January 1977	28 October 1980	15	27	1.800
Elliott, Frank	20 March 1954	10 December 1955	26	61	2.346
Evans, Oswald	31 August 1946	31 August 1946	1	7	7.000
Flack, Doug	2 October 1948	31 January 1953	55	67	1.218
Fryer, Jack	5 September 1903	16 April 1910	170	142	0.835
Gage, Larry	23 April 1949	7 May 1949	3	2	0.666
Gough, Alan	12 September 1992	27 March 1993	3	4	1.333

NAME	FIRST MATCH	LAST MATCH	TOTAL PLAYED	GOALS CONCEDED	AVERAGE
Gregory, John	8 April 1995	8 April 1995	0+1	0	0.000
Grew, Mark (loan)	7 September 1985	21 September 1985	4	5	1.250
Harrison, Lee	3 December 1994	20 April 1996	12+1	13	1.000
Head, Jack	30 December 1899	27 April 1903	66	96	1.454
Hesford, Iain (loan)	26 January 1985	9 February 1985	3	5	1.666
Hewkins, Ken	12 November 1955	10 February 1962	41	101	2.463
Hinton, Ted	2 September 1946	25 September 1948	86	110	1.279
Horne, Will	16 March 1907	27 April 1907	2	5	2.500
Iceton, Jake	30 August 1930	2 April 1934	99	151	1.525
Kelly, Hugh	17 September 1949	6 May 1950	27	33	1.222
Lange, Tony	12 August 1995	31 January 1997	70	94	1.342
Lloyd, David *	18 April 1901	18 April 1901	1	0	0.000
Macedo, Tony	7 December 1957	4 May 1968	391	666	1.703
McClelland, Jack	8 November 1965	19 April 1969	57	117	2.052
McDonald, Hugh	8 November 1913	25 December 1913	8	11	1.375
McKenna, Tom	25 April 1925	17 October 1925	10	26	2.600
Maile, Albert	10 September 1898	2 December 1899	30	49	1.633
Mason, Bill	10 November 1928	3 May 1930	38	68	1.789
Meeson, Arthur	9 March 1929	9 March 1929	1	4	4.000
Mellor, Peter	26 February 1972	20 November 1976	224	239	1.066
Nixon, Wilf	25 December 1912	30 April 1921	29	35	1.206
O'Donnell, Rudolph	27 December 1909	8 January 1910	3	6	2.000
Parks, Tony	2 March 1991	9 March 1991	2	4	2.000
Peyton, Gerry	4 December 1976	3 May 1986	395	501	1.268
Radcliffe, Mark	7 December 1946	28 February 1948	13	25	1.923
Rance, C	19 October 1901	30 November 1901	2	3	1.500
Reynolds, Arthur	23 April 1910	18 April 1925	420	503	1.197
Ronson, Brian	6 March 1954	13 March 1954	2	5	2.500
Seymour, Ian	27 March 1967	19 December 1970	75	120	1.600
Skene, Leslie	3 September 1907	29 March 1910	94	122	1.297
Stannard, Jim	31 January 1981	22 April 1995	430	593	1.379
Taylor, Maik**	18 November 1997	28 December 1997	9	8	0.888
Teale, Richard	21 August 1976	1 January 1977	5	14	2.800
Thompson, Fred	18 November 1905	3 February 1906	5	5	1.000
Tootill, Alf	3 December 1932	1 January 1938	214	306	1.429
Townsend, Martin	2 September 1963	14 September 1963	3	13	4.333
Turner, Hugh	28 August 1937	29 April 1939	71	93	1.309
Underwood, Dave	28 August 1963	28 September 1964	19	26	1.368
Vaughan, John	23 August 1986	2 May 1987	52	91	1.750
Walton, Mark	17 August 1996	1 November 1997	45	41	0.911
Webster, Malcolm	19 December 1969	24 November 1973	104	128	1.230
Whalley, Fred	29 March 1924	21 March 1925	9	12	1.333
Williamson, Brian	21 December 1968	30 August 1969	14	33	2.357

* Normally an outfield player.

** Appearances to the end of 1997

TOP 20 AVERAGES
(Qualification 50 matches)

	APPS	AVERAGE GOALS PER MATCH
Jack Fryer*	170	0.835
Peter Mellor	224	1.066
Arthur Reynolds	420	1.197
Doug Flack	55	1.218
Malcolm Webster	104	1.230
Gerry Peyton	395	1.268
Ted Hinton	86	1.279
Leslie Skene	94	1.297
Hugh Turner	71	1.309
Tony Lange	70	1.342
Jim Stannard	430	1.379
Alf Tootill	214	1.429
Jack Head	66	1.454
Jake Iceton	99	1.525
Ian Seymour	75	1.600
Ian Black	277	1.700
Tony Macedo	391	1.703
John Vaughan	52	1.750
Ernie Beecham	185	1.929
Jack McClelland	57	2.052

* Mainly in Southern League

Having conceded just 41 goals in 45 games, Mark Walton, with an average of 0.911, only just fails to qualify for second place in the table above.

50 OR MORE CONSECUTIVE APPEARANCES

Ernie Beecham	130	1925-26	to	1928-29
Peter Mellor	130	1973-74	to	1975-76
Arthur Reynolds	127	1920-21	to	1923-24
Gerry Peyton	111	1976-77	to	1978-79
Arthur Reynolds	100	1909-10	to	1912-13
Alf Tootill	93	1933-34	to	1935-36
Jim Stannard	89	1987-88	to	1988-89
Jim Stannard	81	1992-93	to	1994-95
Arthur Reynolds	81	1919-20	to	1920-21
Peter Mellor	76	1971-72	to	1973-74
Jim Stannard	70	1990-91	to	1992-93
Tony Macedo	67	1961-62	to	1963-64
Hugh Turner	65	1937-38	to	1938-39
Ian Black	61	1950-51	to	1951-52
Tony Macedo	59	1957-58	to	1958-59
Tony Macedo	58	1964-65	to	1965-66
Malcolm Webster	58	1970-71	to	1971-72
Gerry Peyton	55	1981-82	to	1982-83
Jake Iceton	53	1931-32	to	1932-33
Jack Fryer	52	1905-06	to	1906-07

Above: The inimitable Peter Mellor.

Opposite top: Laurence 'George' Batty.

Opposite bottom: Malcolm Webster all at sea.

Albert Maile	1898
HS Curling	1899
Jack Head	1899
David Lloyd	1901
C Rance	1901
Jack Fryer	1903
Fred Biggar	1903
Henry Clutterbuck	1904
Fred Thompson	1905
Will Horne	1907
Leslie Skene	1907
Herbert Crossthwaite	1908
Rudolph O'Donnell	1909
Arthur Reynolds	1910
Wilf Nixon	1912
Hugh McDonald	1913
Fred Whalley	1924
Leonard Boot	1925
Tom McKenna	1925
Ernie Beecham	1925
Bill Mason	1928
Arthur Meeson	1929
Jake Iceton	1930
Alf Tootill	1932
Leonard Brooks	1936
Hugh Turner	1937
Oswald Evans	1946
Ted Hinton	1946
Mark Radcliffe	1946
Doug Flack	1948

Larry Gage	1949
Hugh Kelly	1949
Ian Black	1950
Brian Ronson	1954
Frank Elliott	1954
Ken Hewkins	1955
Tony Macedo	1957
Dave Underwood	1963
Martin Townsend	1963
Jack McClelland	1965
Ian Seymour	1967
Brian Williamson	1968
Malcolm Webster	1969
Peter Mellor	1972
Richard Teale	1976
Gerry Peyton	1976
Perry Digweed	1977
Jim Stannard	1981
Iain Hesford (loan)	1985
Laurence Batty	1985
Mark Grew (loan)	1985
John Vaughan	1986
Tony Parks	1991
Alan Gough	1992
Lee Harrison	1994
John Gregory (sub)	1995
Tony Lange	1995
Mark Walton	1996
Andre Arendse	1997
Maik Taylor	1997

GOALKEEPERS WHO PLAYED FOR A WHOLE SEASON

	SEASON	LEAGUE/CUP	MATCHES
Jack Head	1902-03	SL2/FAC	19
Arthur Reynolds	1910-11	FL2/FAC	39
	1911-12	FL2/FAC	42
	1921-22	FL2/FAC	45
	1922-23	FL2/FAC	43
Ernie Beecham	1926-27	FL2/FAC	44
	1927-28	FL2/FAC	43
Alf Tootill	1934-35	FL2/FAC	43
Hugh Turner	1938-39	FL2/FAC	44
Ian Black	1950-51	FL1/FAC	47
Tony Macedo	1962-63	FL1/FAC/FLC	47
Peter Mellor	1972-73	FL2/FAC/FLC	47
	1974-75	FL2/FAC/FLC	57
	1975-76	FL2/FAC/FLC	46
Gerry Peyton	1977-78	FL2/FAC/FLC	45
	1982-83	FL2/FAC/FLC	49
Jim Stannard	1987-88	BL3/FAC/LCC	51
	1991-92	BL3/FAC/RLC	49
	1993-94	EL2/FAC/CCC	51

Arthur Reynolds missed only one match in the 1923-24 season.
Alf Tootill missed only one match in both the 1935-36 and 1936-37 seasons.
Jim Stannard missed only one match (against Gillingham!) in the 1988-89 season.

Above: Gerry Peyton.

Below: Mark Walton.

Key to competitions:
SL   Southern League
FAC   Football Association Cup
FL   Football League
FLC   Football League Cup
BL   Barclays League
LCC   Littlewoods Challenge Cup
RLC   Rumbelows League Cup
EL   Endsleigh League
CCC   Coca-Cola Cup

GOALKEEPERS WITH CLEAN SHEETS IN FOUR OR MORE CONSECUTIVE MATCHES

Jack Head	5	28 March 1902	to	19 April 1902
Jack Head	6	20 September 1902	to	25 October 1902
Jack Fryer	4	22 April 1905	to	2 September 1905
Jack Fryer	4*	10 March 1906	to	31 March 1906
Jack Fryer	7*	14 April 1906	to	22 September 1906
Jack Fryer	4	3 November 1906	to	24 November 1906
Jack Fryer	4	2 April 1907	to	20 April 1907
Arthur Reynolds	4	25 April 1914	to	9 September 1914
Arthur Reynolds	4	20 September 1919	to	11 October 1919
Arthur Reynolds	4	20 March 1920	to	3 April 1920
Arthur Reynolds	5	4 February 1922	to	4 March 1922
Arthur Reynolds	6	3 March 1923	to	31 March 1923
Arthur Reynolds	5	5 April 1924	to	22 April 1924
Ted Hinton	5	6 March 1948	to	27 March 1948
Ian Black	4	6 April 1957	to	20 April 1957
Tony Macedo	4	2 March 1963	to	23 March 1963
Peter Mellor	4	22 September 1973	to	6 October 1973
Peter Mellor	4	23 March 1974	to	6 April 1974
Gerry Peyton	4	9 April 1977	to	23 April 1977
Gerry Peyton	4	20 January 1981	to	6 February 1981
Jim Stannard	6	28 February 1992	to	20 March 1992
Jim Stannard	4	10 April 1993	to	24 April 1993
Mark Walton	4**	8 March 1997	to	31 March 1997
Mark Walton	4**	19 April 1997	to	9 August 1997

* Had Jack Fryer not allowed Northampton Town to put one past him on 7 April 1906, he would have gone 12 consecutive Southern League Division One games without conceding a goal.
** Mark Walton kept eight clean sheets in the last 11 matches of the 1996-97 season, and followed this up with another one on the opening day of 1997-98.

CAPPED KEEPERS

Although a number of Fulham goalkeepers won international caps at youth level, none have (so far!) won full international honours for England, Scotland or Wales while playing for Fulham. The table below therefore lists Fulham's Irish Internationals.

	COUNTRY	MATCHES	GOALS CONCEDED	AVERAGE
Ted Hinton	Northern Ireland	5	5	1.00
Hugh Kelly	Northern Ireland	2	9	4.50
Jack McClelland	Northern Ireland	1	1	1.00
Gerry Peyton	Republic of Ireland	20+1	26	1.24

In addition, Andre Arendse has played for South Africa since joining Fulham.

Two of the more unusual keepers to have guarded the Cottagers' goal. Malcolm Macdonald (above) stood in for Ian Seymour against Southampton reserves in March 1969, while Kevin Lock (right) deputised for the injured Gerry Peyton some years later.